Team Challenges

170+ Group Activities

to Build Cooperation, Communication, and Creativity

Kris Bordessa

Zephyr Press

Chicago

Library of Congress Cataloging-in-Publication Data
Bordessa, Kris.
  Team challenges : group activities to build cooperation, communication,
and creativity / Kris Bordessa.-- 1st ed.
      p. cm.
  ISBN 1-56976-201-5
1. Problem-based learning. 2. Group problem solving. 3. Critical
thinking. 4. Cooperation. I. Title.
  LB1027.42.B67 2006
  371.39--dc22
                                                    2005013741

Cover and interior design: Rattray Design

© 2006 by Kris Bordessa
All rights reserved
Published by Zephyr Press
An imprint of Chicago Review Press, Incorporated
814 North Franklin Street
Chicago, Illinois 60610
ISBN-13: 978-1-56976-201-1
ISBN-10: 1-56976-201-5
Printed in the United States of America

Contents

Acknowledgments   v

Introduction   vii

1   **Creativity, Cooperation, and Communication**   1
    What Are They Good For?

2   **Get It Together**   9
    Gather Your Group and Prepare for Some Fun

3   **Everything but the Kitchen Sink**   21
    Commonly Used Materials and Their Uncommon Uses

4   **Tiny Tasks**   31
    Warm Up with These Quick Activities

5   **Talk It Up**   37
    Discuss Options, Share Ideas, and Make Connections

6   **Construction for the Whole Crew**   65
    Building Towers, Bridges, Roads, and More

7   **Move It!**   159
    Physical Activities

8   **Show Me the Funny**   213
    Improv Hilarity at Its Best

9   **Trouble with Tasks?**   265
    Working Through Some Difficult Spots

Resources   271
Creative-Problem-Solving Programs for Youth

Acknowledgments

As a DestiNation Imagination team manager, I had trouble finding suitable team-building activities for my groups; as a writer, I was brash enough to take on the project of creating them. The folks at Zephyr Press took me seriously, and in an amazingly smooth process, made it happen.

My fabulous teams—Double Trouble, The Time Raiders, The Black Knights, The Windboards, and CPWS (Cheezy People Wearing Speedos)—have inspired me, tested my limits, and made me laugh until I cried again and again. No matter how I envisioned each task presented to them, they always surprised me with their clever and unorthodox solutions.

I'm ever grateful to the friends and family who have cheered me on, proofread pages, and talked me through many frustrations—you rock!

But most importantly, I've had the support of my husband and two boys. They have become accustomed to scattered, precariously stacked piles of materials that will some day—some day—become an eight-minute-long presentation that will test the limits of imagination as can openers pull Trojan Horses to victory, foam pads become armor for the devious Red Knights, and Ayers Rock is transformed into the Golden Gate Bridge. My guys have been patient as I completed this book, graciously (well, most of the time) accepting countless dinners of cold cereal, days without clean socks, and many, many bad hair days. I love you guys.

Introduction

Working with children can be one of life's most rewarding experiences. It's also quite a lot like herding cats. Just when you think you've got everyone's attention, you find that a stray has wandered off in chase of a butterfly.

As a group leader for several youth organizations, I've experienced the difficulty of encouraging a group of children to move in the same direction while still respecting each individual's needs. I've watched as the simple act of compromise has reduced a frustrated child to tears. And I've seen how, with a bit of guidance, support, and an introduction to creative problem solving, kids can learn to work as a group toward a common goal.

In my role as group leader, I used to find myself constantly in need of new material. I searched my memory for the activities—campfire skits, relay races, challenges to see who could build the tallest tower or longest bridge, competitions for the most creative cabin decoration, blindfolded lipstick application—that I had loved during my own participation in 4-H and other youth programs, and I shared these childhood favorites with my teams. But, while those activities from long ago were a good start, I needed more.

Those fun childhood activities, as well as others that I've learned more recently, have compelled me to expand on those ideas and develop a resource of easy-to-implement activities that will keep kids laughing, having fun, and learning the benefits of teamwork, all at the same time.

Team challenges offer parents and teachers an easy way to share the concept of creative problem solving with children. Through these simple, hands-on activities, kids can experiment with building methods, discover new uses for everyday items, try on new personas, and learn to express some unusual ideas as they work toward solving a problem as a team. Your group will learn to work together on projects such as creating a bridge out of marshmallows, straws, and paper or building as tall a tower as possible from toothpicks, raisins, cardboard, and balloons.

Sure, you say. My group could do that. But could they do it in just five minutes? And will their structure hold weight? The tasks found in this book will challenge the minds of the young and the young at heart to come up with a creative solution within specific guidelines and time limits.

Team challenges offer kids a chance to see firsthand how crucial teamwork is to success. By working together on short tasks during each class meeting or team session, participants will begin to understand what it means to work cooperatively with other people.

Grammar school students, high school bands, student council members, pep squads, and even siblings—all of these kids will learn valuable lessons through their participation in team challenges. Whether your group is a team working to solve a long-term problem in an organized competition, a casual youth group, or a group of students, family, and friends, utilizing *Team Challenges* will encourage cooperation and provide ideas for jump-starting creativity and fostering cooperation.

The early chapters of *Team Challenges* offer a look at team building and how best to implement the activities in this book with your group. Chapter 1 gives a brief introduction to cooperation, communication, and creativity and how learning these skills will benefit kids, both now and later in life. Chapter 2 will help teachers and team leaders determine the best way to utilize the tasks with their groups. Most of the materials used in *Team Challenges* are simple household items or cast-offs; in chapter 3 you'll find a list of good materials to keep on hand for last-minute activities as well as potential substitutes.

With this information, you'll be ready to start introducing team challenges to your group. Chapter 4 is a good place to start: Tiny Tasks are simple challenges that require a minimum of materials and have very simple instructions.

The rest of the tasks in this book include several different types of challenges. In chapter 5, your group will "talk it up" with verbal tasks. By exploring simple, thought-provoking questions, participants will learn to brainstorm and share answers beyond the norm. In chapter 6 your team's construction skills will be tested as participants utilize an assortment of household and recycled items to build structures or models to fit within certain criteria. While some structures must hold weight, others may need to span a certain distance. The tasks in chapter 7 get teams moving with activities that instill a feeling of trust and encourage clear communication. Participants will work together to accomplish specific goals, depending upon their teammates to help them through a sticky situation. Many of the tasks in chapter 8 incorporate a bit of role-playing and acting, as participants utilize props and their creativity to develop a short production, portray a scene, or create a solution to a hypothetical problem.

With practice, your teams will excel at solving these challenges creatively, but in the beginning, they may have some difficulties in learning to work together. Chapter 9 addresses potential trouble spots and offers ideas for smoothing the way.

While the tasks differ in nature, they all have one thing in common: the solutions must come quickly. Teammates often have only a few minutes to discuss their plan and several more to implement it. This teaches them to communicate quickly, effectively, and without conflict. Discussions following the completion of the tasks allow team members to analyze what worked, what didn't, and how they could improve their performance next time. With regular use of these tasks, participants will stretch their knowledge and abilities, learning how to solve a variety of problems.

Every task included in this book requires participants to think creatively, cooperate with one another, and communicate clearly in order to complete the given task. Young people with skills such as these are an asset to their peers, easy to work with, and impressive to watch in action. The ability to work with a team and think outside the box will serve these kids well, not only with their team, but also in the future. Working together creatively to solve the tasks in this book will help provide kids with many of the tools they need to succeed in life.

1

Creativity, Cooperation, and Communication

What Are They Good For?

Creativity

What makes a person creative? Is it the ability to wield a paintbrush, bringing an image to life on canvas? Is it the ability to sculpt clay into a breathtaking likeness of a living being? Is it composing music? Is it a gardener's ability to landscape in colors that flow through the garden like a vivid sunset?

People will readily give Monet, Beethoven, and Van Gogh credit for being creative souls, but likening one's own creativity to that of such revered figures is usually unthinkable. In fact, many people will deny having any creative ability at all. *Artistic* creativity is what most people think of when they hear the word *creative*, and the artistic genius of Monet, Beethoven, and Van Gogh is indeed rare. But creativity isn't just about art. What, then, *is* it about?

Creativity is a thought process that allows for much experimentation. It's a fresh way of looking at old situations. It's a unique perspective. It's the ability to perceive situations or our surroundings in a new and unusual manner. Our world is filled with creative individuals—sometimes where we'd least expect them. When Charles Menches ran out of dishes in which to serve his ice cream at the 1904 World's Fair, he didn't panic: he created the ice cream cone. And when Bette Nesmith Graham, a single mother, went to work as a typist to support her children in 1951, she found she wasn't always accurate. To remedy the situation, she created what she called Mistake Out. Twenty-eight years later she sold her invention—renamed White Out—to the Gillette Corporation for $47.5 million.

Think about other innovations that shape our daily lives. Thomas Edison was thinking outside the box, way before the term was cool, when he lit up our nights. The world we live in would look quite different today without Bill Gates and Henry Ford. And without creativity, we would never have known the Chia Pet, the Swiffer, or the Clapper. Creative people thought of many of the items we take for granted today. They imagined an entirely new invention or expanded on an old one to create a completely new idea.

Creative thinkers of the future will have the opportunity to solve many problems—and there are plenty to go around. The search for a cure to the common cold has been fruitless. The coils on refrigerators get dusty, toilet seats are left up, and diapers still need to be changed. When some creative soul comes along with a solution for these problems, our world will indeed change for the better.

"Why didn't I think of that?" How many times have you said that to yourself upon seeing a new product or clever idea? People just like you dreamed up these innovations, but they had something else going for them: they were creative problem solvers.

Creative thinking isn't only about inventing products, though. Attacking a problem from a different angle and coming up with a solution can also result in successful plans and ideas that will benefit all involved. For years, our nation has struggled with difficult problems that won't be solved until someone thinks of a new solution. The energy crisis comes and goes without ever reaching a suitable conclusion. Our waste continues to overwhelm us, filling up landfills in spite of our recycling efforts. Poverty levels are high, and homelessness is much more common than it should be in our wealthy nation. Just imagine the problems that future generations could overcome if parents and teachers learned to guide children and young adults toward creative thinking skills!

If there's any doubt in your mind about the desirability of a creative mind, consider this: classified ads are rife with employers seeking "creative self-starters" and prospective college students are encouraged to show creativity in their enrollment applications. Kids well versed in the art of creative thinking will have a jump start in life.

Teaching a group of kids to problem solve creatively is a task well worth undertaking. It is also a job that takes patience, tenacity, and some creativity of your own. If you've picked up this book, it is likely that you understand the need for adults to encourage creativity in young people. But how do you go about teaching kids to think creatively?

Creativity can't be taught in the same manner that math, for example, can be taught. There are no facts to memorize, no right or wrong answers. Creativity is difficult to quantify. In a classroom setting, students who correctly answer questions or solve problems are rewarded with high marks. But, in life, once we leave the confines of the school setting, very few of the decisions we make have a single, correct answer. Life offers plenty of options along the way, minus an instruction manual or answer key. As in life, with creative thinking there is seldom a *right* answer. Creativity is a thought process that can be encouraged through open-ended learning activities, discussions, and challenges. Enter *Team Challenges*. Each task in this book provides the opportunity to expand the mind and solve problems in multiple ways, all while having fun.

Fostering creativity among children and young adults is something that should be a priority for every parent, teacher, and group leader. Kids will grow into creative adults only if we provide opportunities for exploring a variety of possibilities and allow them to express their ideas in a setting free of judgment, ridicule, or comparison. Creative thinking is a skill that can be encouraged in every person on earth. And well it should be. Creative thinkers are able to freely express unique ideas, solve problems, and act in a resourceful manner, all of which are assets to society.

Cooperation

Remember back in grade school, when report cards happily proclaimed, "Works well with others"? Getting along with our peers was an important part of our day. As adults, we no longer depend on such a proclamation; however, our interactions with others do earn us a reputation that often precedes us. The adult version of "works well with others" is a glowing recommendation from a friend or coworker. People who are easy to get along with, dependable, and considerate of others' ideas will naturally gain the respect of the people they deal with.

Teaching kids to work together as a group maximizes their understanding of teamwork, creates a feeling of belonging and trust, and encourages creative problem solving. Students have the opportunity to learn as part of a group when they work together toward a common goal. Working as a team, they learn that each participant has strengths and weaknesses. Recognizing each person's limitations and abilities, as well as their own, encourages participants to depend upon and trust one another.

Regardless of your team's makeup, eliminating dissention among groups is a key element of these challenges. Without creativity, cooperation, and communication, problems can seem bigger than they really are. Differences of opinion are to be expected, but by utilizing the communication aspect of team challenges, teammates will learn to calmly and respectfully share their ideas and move toward actually solving the problem at hand.

Of course, this isn't always as simple as it sounds. Two confident team members can butt heads if they both think their solution is the only correct solution. With regular engagement in team challenges, participants will learn to see that each task presents a number of different possibilities for a solution. There is no such thing as a correct answer, since the problems presented can be solved any number of ways.

Just as that vocal, natural-born leader can wreak havoc on team tranquility, an overly quiet child can hinder the team's success as well; if ideas are not verbalized, the team will not have the opportunity to try them. Cooperation requires participation by everyone on the team and consideration of all viewpoints. In working together toward a common goal, groups may toss out some unusual possibilities for solving a task. Team members must be prepared to acknowledge all ideas as potential solutions, even those that might be considered a bit wacky.

A group of middle school boys I recently worked with was searching for a way to make an invention move across the floor. After much discussion and many unsuccessful attempts, the boys came up with the idea of modifying an electric can opener to pull their invention across the floor. It worked. With a little thought and creativity, *every* suggestion has the potential to become a great solution.

Teamwork encourages participants to work on conflict resolution skills as well. There is bound to be some disagreement about the best way to solve some of the tasks presented here. Participants will learn to work quickly through differences of opinion and to accept that all of the members of the team have valid suggestions.

Have you ever heard the phrase "There's no *I* in *team*"? In order to complete the tasks in this book, teams must collaborate to come up with a solution that is agreeable to the entire group. Teammates will need to learn to trust one another's fairness and to explain their opinions clearly and concisely; within the time limits imposed on each task, there is little room for arguing about the best solution. Students will quickly learn that spending three minutes of their valuable time debating the merits of each idea is ultimately going to interfere with the completion of their task. This is not to say that there won't be differences of opinion initially. Just as with anything else in life, learning to work cooperatively takes practice.

In short order, the group will realize that every member of the team is a valuable part of the final solution and that competition against one's own teammates is counterproductive. Without the efforts of the entire group, the team is working with a handicap. In order for teams to excel, all members must collaborate on an innovative idea to solve the problem creatively.

The fast-paced nature of the tasks in this book requires a bit of risk taking. There isn't time to debate the very best course of action before jumping in to solve the problem. Rather, teams must get immediately to work, problem solve along the way, and incorporate past learning experiences in order to come up with the best possible solution—quickly.

Communication

Smoke signals. War drums. Cave paintings. Runes. Hieroglyphs. Sign language. Newspapers. The Pony Express. Telegraph. Telegrams. Telephone. The postal service. Federal Express. Fax. E-mail. Cell phones. Instant messaging. Chat rooms.

The methods we use to communicate may have changed over the years, but the basic principles remain the same. We talk, others listen, and vice-versa. In modern-day life, we have countless avenues for conveying our needs, desires, or dreams. We communicate with other people every day. From our good morning nod to ordering lunch; from greeting the bus driver to waving hello; from asking for directions to saying good night, communication is an inevitable part of our day. Honing our communication skills can help us avoid conflicts, improve relationships, and increase understanding between groups of people. In spite of the ever-increasing means of communication, there is no guarantee that these methods are effective. In these days of modern technology, it is still a *human* obligation to communicate clearly.

True communication involves listening, comprehension, and the ability to convey an idea clearly. While we all have some basic communication skills, this doesn't necessarily mean that we are good at it. Sure, we talk to one another; however, if our ideas aren't articulated clearly, there is potential for miscommunication.

Speaking is only one half of successful communication. Listening—and comprehending the words we hear—completes the communication cycle. In order to make certain we hear pertinent information, it is crucial to listen as people speak. Adults in the midst of an exciting conversation have a tendency to get caught up in the moment. How many times have you participated in a conversation that felt more like a competition to finish a thought than a calm exchange of ideas? Instead of focusing on what to say next, we need to learn to turn off the dictation in our heads and simply listen. While the average person speaks at about 130 words per minute, our thinking speed is about 500 words per minute, meaning that our brains are often jumping ahead of the conversation.

The language skills of humans improve over time: babies evolve from crying for attention to grunting and pointing and finally to individual words. Stringing together words to form sentences is the culmination of long months of listening and practice. But as we gain the ability to communicate verbally, should we stop learning how to improve our communication skills?

Clear communication is crucial in every aspect of our lives, from relationships to careers. Effective communication allows us to confidently express our opinions, understand another point of view, and give accurate instructions.

The only way to learn to communicate more clearly is to practice. Team challenges provide the opportunity to practice communication skills in a nonthreatening setting and to assess within minutes what worked and what didn't. As teammates regularly work through each task, they will begin to see how effective communication skills can aid in successfully tackling problems.

Working within a group to solve a problem or come up with alternative ideas enhances the creative process, encourages cooperation, and fosters clear communication. The life skills learned through team challenges will benefit children and young adults, now and in the future. The divergent thinking skills learned through team challenges are invaluable for students. Creativity, cooperation, and communication are assets that will help our children thrive not only in a competitive work environment, but also in their daily lives.

2

Get It Together

Gather Your Group and Prepare for Some Fun

Team Challenges requires a willingness to step beyond the regular realm of learning activities and into the world of creative problem solving. The activities in this book encourage participants to explore the possibilities for solving challenging problems. Exactly what *is* the best way to build a tower out of newspaper and tape? Or the best way to portray a movie character with only a paper bag for a prop? Adults and the kids they work with will appreciate that, with this type of task, there *isn't* one correct way to solve the problem. The opportunity to solve these problems in countless ways makes these activities fun for all involved.

With the regular use of team challenges, your group will learn to use creative problem-solving skills, work together, and overcome communication difficulties in order to solve some interesting dilemmas. Kids will also learn successful building methods, increase divergent thinking skills, and gain insight into the skillful use of some unusual materials. There is an amazing amount of flexibility in each task, but some general guidelines will help you facilitate a successful experience for your entire group or classroom.

Who Can Use *Team Challenges*?

The short answer is *anyone*. Regardless of age or ability, team challenges are a fun way to expose kids to the concept that together, we're better.

Whether you are a team leader of an organized group that will ultimately participate in a competition, a leader of a youth organization, or a teacher trying to encourage cooperation among your students, the tasks within the covers of this book will provide ideas for jump-starting creativity and fostering cooperation among your group.

Assembling a Team

So, what exactly is a *team*? For this book, I've used the term to indicate any small group of people that wants to learn to think creatively, work together toward a common goal, and have fun. Most of the tasks in this book work best with groups of three to eight, though many of them will work with larger groups as well.

If you are conducting team challenges in a classroom setting and dividing students into several smaller groups, I would recommend maintaining the same groups for a number of sessions. Participants will find that coming up with a creative solution is easier as they begin to recognize and rely on their teammates' strengths.

Teams working toward a long-term goal, such as those with DestiNation Imagination or Odyssey of the Mind, will work together for an extended amount of time, sometimes coming together year after year. After a while, as these groups begin to anticipate one another's moves and to understand the different strengths and personalities of each team member, they will find that the solution to each task comes more easily. One team member, for instance, may be especially suited to guiding the team through a difficult building task, but may find improvisational tasks to be more of a challenge. Learning to recognize each team member's strengths will allow teams to come up with the best solution possible, based on all of the team members' ideas.

Newly formed groups or groups that change on a regular basis may not move in such a fluid manner. However, one benefit of rotating groups is that kids will learn to be flexible about how to solve each task with a variety of teammates.

At first, the concept of working as a team to solve each problem may feel foreign, and kids will need time to learn that each idea has merit. But with a little practice, they will be able to quickly sort through the numerous ideas offered and choose a plan of action that will lead the group as a whole on to success.

Make It a Positive Environment

Successful collaboration comes in a positive setting. A nonjudgmental group is essential to seeking out the most creative solutions, whether during team challenges or in the future challenges that life has a tendency to present.

Creating a positive environment in which teammates can share their silliest ideas is crucial to successful creative thinking. We've all seen kids who are ridiculed for their every move. A child in this situation tends to stop participating in discussions simply to avoid the teasing. With team challenges—and some adult guidance—hesitant children will learn to voice their ideas without the fear of ridicule. Other participants will come to discover that everybody has something to offer. The wonderful thing about kids working as a team to problem solve is that, over time, they will learn that the only way to be successful is to work with one another rather than to compete for recognition.

When a participant offers an idea that seems silly or impossible, as a leader you can help diffuse the situation. Call a time-out during the task or wait until the task is complete, but be sure to lead the team back to that silly suggestion and encourage the kids to think about how it could have been part of the solution. Could the idea have been altered somehow? Would a portion of the idea have worked? Maybe the first version of the idea was ludicrous, but with a little further thought, it could have been a creative solution.

> **Team Tip**
>
> *Keep a pen and notebook handy to jot down comments as the group works. This way, you can provide the team with feedback once the task is completed.*

To help your team members understand what is expected of them and what makes a positive setting, give them some guidelines. I've listed a few of my own rules for a positive environment below. It's important to note that these rules apply to all adults involved as well. Creating a positive environment is impossible if the adults refuse to follow the same guidelines as the team.

Team Players Do

- Use encouraging words, such as "Great idea!" "How could we make that work?" and "Let me help you"
- Remind the group of the necessity to be positive, without putting anyone down
- Listen to all ideas offered
- Work toward the most creative solution

Team Players Don't

- Ridicule teammates or their ideas
- Exclude other people or their ideas
- Use judgmental statements, such as "That's stupid!" or "That will never work"
- Grab materials from teammates
- Insist that their solution is the best
- Place blame on other participants when something goes wrong

Every team member is a valuable addition to the final solution. If one participant is excluded from solving the problem, the team is essentially short one member. As a leader, you can gently remind the team after the task that a team effort means the *entire* team. Ask the teammates what they could have done to encourage participation from everyone and gently ask hesitant team members what would make them more likely to help with the group's solution.

The Role of Team Leader

Your role in presenting the tasks is that of a facilitator. You must make sure you understand the activity, assemble the materials, provide an ideal working area, and present the tasks to the team. You *must not* get involved in the team's solution in any way. Giving suggestions, sharing ideas, and leading the team to a solution will interfere with the kids' ability to solve the task themselves. If your group is going to learn from the completion of each task, the lesson should be one of discovery.

The most important aspect of implementing team challenges is that teachers and team leaders must allow participants to solve the problem in their own manner, without adult criticism or suggestions. At first, doing so will challenge the comfort level of many adults, as they learn to step back and allow the group to make mistakes and learn from them. Watching as kids struggle to understand a concept that is basic to most adults is difficult, but giving advice during a task is absolutely not allowed.

Things can and will go wrong. You can certainly restart your team members if something happens that sends them into a tailspin. However, learning to cope with tough situations is important, so make sure you aren't rescuing your team every time things get a little dicey.

During one of my teams' attempts to solve a task outdoors, the wind picked up and materials began to blow away. One of the parents began to interrupt the participants in the middle of their solution to move them inside and out of the wind. I stopped her, explaining that the wind was simply creating a bit more of a challenge for the team. Ultimately, the team figured out how to overcome windswept materials and solved the task in the face of adversity.

There will be tasks that teams are unable to solve successfully. Allow them to wrestle with these difficult problems. They will discover what works and what doesn't and will learn from their mistakes and frustrations.

Presenting the tasks:

1. Read the task to make sure you understand it.
2. Assemble the necessary materials.
3. Set up the task according to the instructions.
4. Gather your team.
5. Read the list of construction materials (when relevant) and team instructions aloud.
6. Ask if there are any questions.
7. Read the task (minus the materials list) a second time for clarification purposes.
8. Set a timer and give a start signal.

Once the team begins a task, step back and observe. The most important part of your job now is to be quiet. You'll need to watch the team's performance and provide feedback for the team following the completion of the task. It's helpful to take notes about what you see, so that you can remember to share it with the team following the task. You'll read more about follow-up later in the chapter.

How Often Should I Present These Tasks?

Teams should have the opportunity to try out new tasks on a regular basis. Doing one task is like doing one push-up. Sure, you completed the activity, but there isn't much room for improvement when you only make one attempt. The more regularly you include team challenges in your schedule, the more comfortable your team will become with creative problem solving. At the very minimum, complete one task a week. If you can manage several per week or one task per day, all the better.

The Solutions

While team challenges are simple to use with a wide variety of groups and assorted ages, the tasks differ from many familiar activities in that there isn't one *correct* answer to a single task in this book.

For example, in one of the tasks in chapter 8, the team is instructed to create a superhero. Nothing in the instructions tells the team what form the superhero must take. So, while some teams may whip up a miniature superhero from the materials provided, others may use the materials to create a costume and transform one member of the group into a superhero. Two different solutions to the same problem!

When you first implement these tasks, students accustomed to grades and assessments may express concern about how well they did. They will quickly come to understand that the team is really the best judge of that. Discussing their solution after each session, along with various ways they could have improved their communication and teamwork, will allow kids to gain an understanding of how best to tackle future problems.

Children just learning the concept of creative problem solving and working as a team will at first come up with a very basic solution. As they continue to learn through actively solving the problems presented here, their solutions will begin to reflect bolder ideas, more daring characters, and more successful collaborations.

What About Timing?

The time limit given with each challenge is included to teach teams to solve problems quickly, cooperatively, and decisively. If your team is young or struggling with the short time frame given with each task, feel free to add a minute or two to the allotted time until the kids begin to grasp the concept of working together quickly to solve a task.

Sometimes, a team's task is still incomplete when time expires. This is OK! As teammates continue to improve their ability to assess the problem and communicate about possible solutions, their time management skills will improve as well.

Aren't the Tasks a Little Vague?

The tasks in this book *are* a little bit vague, but that's not an error, it's intentional. In addition to requiring teams to work together toward solving a solution, the tasks also require participants to listen carefully to instructions and to interpret them in a creative way. Tell your team members that, if the instructions don't say that they *can't* do something, then they can—as long as it is safe! For kids accustomed to following rules and doing work that must look a certain way, whether it's a report or a science fair project, this might be a difficult concept to grasp. But the whole idea is that with team challenges, kids will learn to think creatively and come up with a unique solution to each challenge.

Assessment

At the completion of each task, have the kids assess their solution. Ask each participant to note one positive thing that happened or worked well and to share one thing that could stand improvement next time.

For your part, you are obligated to observe the way they handled the situation or problem and to be prepared to offer some thoughts after they have completed the challenge. Did they totally forget one part of the instructions? A reminder to listen carefully before they proceed might be in order. Did one participant stand by and watch, without participating at all? Let the team know that one person not participating means one less person contributing—and everyone has something to contribute!

Make your discussion brief; a few quick comments or questions will serve the group better than a long and boring dialogue. Ask the kids some questions to get them thinking about what worked for them and what didn't. Remind the participants that team players work together toward an agreeable solution. Present one or two questions from the following list after each task to get the teammates thinking about how to improve their performance:

- Did everyone on the team contribute to the solution?
- What can you do to encourage every team member to participate?
- Was there anything that you forgot to do?
- Did everyone on the team share at least one idea for solving the problem?
- Did you have any problems with communication?
- How could you have improved your solution?
- What would you do the same way next time?
- Is there another way you could have done it?
- How well do you think you solved this problem?

This is a good opportunity to teach kids to share how they feel about a situation, rather than making accusations. Instead of "He keeps grabbing things from me!" they can try, "It's frustrating when somebody takes something from me before I get a chance to try my idea."

Once the participants have had a chance to assess their solution, you can share your own feedback with them from the Team Tally (see below).

Scoring

Most of the activities in this book include a Team Tally. With this scoring system, teachers and team leaders can provide feedback for the teammates on their creativity, cooperation, and communication. It's important to note that the scores will not be based on the accuracy of a solution. Remember, with team challenges there is no such thing as a correct answer! Rather, the scores are completely subjective. Your job is to observe the kids as they attempt to solve the task and to take notes on both positive and negative aspects of their path to a solution. Take all of these things into consideration as you choose an appropriate score, from one to ten, ten being the best score possible.

In addition to the Team Tallies presented with the individual tasks, you'll also find reproducible scoring sheets at the end of this chapter (page 19) that can be used to assess each team's solution. These reproducible sheets include spaces to record scores for creativity, cooperation, and communication, along with a blank space for noting bonus points. You'll need to write in the appropriate bonus score, as these vary by challenge. Use these reproducible tallies as a way to track your team's progress over time.

When assessing your team's success, your judgment should be fair and address amazing effort, difficulties, or exceptionally creative solutions. While it's not going to serve the team members well to always achieve a high score, neither will it serve them to be harshly critiqued. The Team Tally with each task is simply meant as a measuring stick for the team members. If they are consistently getting low marks for their creativity, they may wish to address this. One way is to have the team repeat the same challenge a number of times, each time coming up with new uses for the same materials.

Bonus points are possible for many of the challenges and are meant to encourage teams to push for the best possible solution. It's easy enough to build a tower, but if the kids know that they can earn bonus points for every inch of height, they will do their best to make the tower as tall as possible. Solving team challenges shouldn't be about coming up with the easy solution—anybody can do that! Kids who use team challenges regularly will learn to test the limits of their abilities and to, on occasion, risk a low score in an attempt to achieve an exceptionally high score.

What if you don't want to give your group a score following the task? No problem. Skip it. The tasks in this book are meant to encourage creativity, cooperation, and communication. If you use these activities with your group regularly, these skills will come with or without the use of the scoring system. I've worked with kids who clamored to find out what their final score was and others who simply didn't care—they were content just to enjoy the activity. The scoring system should inspire your team members to stretch the bounds of their abilities. If you find that the scoring system causes them to worry more about a high score than coming up with a clever solution, then, by all means, leave the scoring out.

Team Tally

	1	2	3	4	5	6	7	8	9	10
Creativity										
Communication										
Cooperation										

Bonus points:

Total points:

Team Tally

	1	2	3	4	5	6	7	8	9	10
Creativity										
Communication										
Cooperation										

Bonus points:

Total points:

Team Tally

	1	2	3	4	5	6	7	8	9	10
Creativity										
Communication										
Cooperation										

Bonus points:

Total points:

3

Everything but the Kitchen Sink

*Commonly Used Materials and Their
Uncommon Uses*

The construction materials used in each team challenge are, for the most part, basic household supplies and castoffs. After assembling a few tasks for your group, you'll begin to think twice before you throw away items such as corks and bottle caps; these items are quickly elevated from trash status to the materials with which your team will excel.

Each team challenge includes a complete list of necessary materials, making it a snap to put together the activities. On occasion, you may find yourself missing some items from the list. Not to worry; in most cases there are some easy substitutions that work just as well.

On the following pages, you'll find listed the more common materials used in team challenges, along with some of their potential uses. Of course, odds are that a creative team will bypass the expected uses and amaze you with unique solutions. Possible substitutions for some of these common materials are also included.

Aluminum Foil

The malleable properties of aluminum foil make it a great material for sculpting. It also works to connect items together or to create a water-safe vessel. In most tasks that call for aluminum foil, only aluminum foil will do.

Possible substitutes: Newspaper, plastic grocery bags, or plastic wrap.

Balloons

Used as precarious tower footings or as flotation devices, balloons can add fun to many tasks. Make certain that you have extras on hand, in case of popped balloons. Avoid oddly shaped balloons, unless you really want to give your team a challenge.

Possible substitutes: Small beach balls, plastic balls, rubber balls, or—for flotation purposes—short lengths cut from a foam swimming pool noodle.

Balls

The tasks in this book use a variety of balls: tennis balls, ping-pong balls, beach balls, and marbles all make an appearance. Take a trip to your nearest sports club or golf course to find out if they sell used balls inexpensively. If you need to substitute, try to find a ball that is roughly the same size and weight as the one called for in the task.

Possible substitutes: Wiffle balls, Super Balls, rubber balls, Styrofoam balls, or golf balls. Balloons make good substitutes for a beach ball.

Bandage Strips

By using bandages as connectors in team challenges, you add the extra element of unwrapping the bandages. Who will do it? What method is the most effective?

Possible substitutes: Masking tape, sticky dots, mailing labels, or sticky notes.

Binder Clips

Stronger than regular paper clips, binder clips are great for holding inventions together. They can also be used as weights or counterweights or as springs to launch an item.

Possible substitutes: Clothespins, paper clips, or hair clips.

Buckets

Commonly used as a place to deposit items that the team must move, buckets can easily be replaced with a number of items. Just take into consideration the size of the item being deposited and the height of the container.

Possible substitutes: Bowls, plastic tubs, or flowerpots.

Cardboard Tubes

Cardboard tubes are easy to come by—save tubes from paper towel rolls or gift wrap. The obvious use for cardboard tubes is as supports, but tubes can also be used to guide moving objects or they can be cut in half lengthwise to create troughs.

Possible substitutes: Short lengths of PVC pipe, paper rolled into tubes, or tissue boxes.

Corks

You'll find corks called for in some of the water-based challenges, in which case their intended use is as a flotation device. They also work as connectors to secure materials together when used in conjunction with toothpicks or paper clips.

Possible substitutes: Styrofoam peanuts, pieces of Styrofoam trays, Styrofoam balls, ping-pong balls, or watertight film canisters.

Drinking Straws

Straws are used frequently as materials for team challenges. Straight straws are the best choice for building, but in a pinch, flexible straws do work. You can give flexible straws to your team as is for a bigger challenge or you can trim off the flexible part before you start. Straws make great supports and are easy to use for spanning a distance. They also work as an axis or for adding length or height. No connectors? No problem! Straws can be connected end-to-end by cutting a short slit into one end. This allows the cut end of one straw to slip inside the uncut end of another. Again, give your team members some time to discover this solution themselves.

Possible substitutes: Dried spaghetti noodles, toothpicks, Popsicle sticks, or pretzel sticks.

Index Cards

In some tasks, teams must create a structure that holds something. Index cards work well as a platform for holding weights or other required elements. Index cards can also be used as supports or to add length or height.

Possible substitutes: Playing cards, magazine subscription cards, or recycled greeting cards.

Marshmallows

If you've ever toasted marshmallows, you know all about their sticky quality. Oddly enough, it may take kids some time to realize that tearing the marshmallows open provides an alternative type of adhesive. But don't give up the secret too quickly: give them the opportunity to discover this on their own. Marshmallows also work well as connectors when used with straws, paper clips, or spaghetti noodles.

Possible substitutes: Raisins, sticky dots, Styrofoam peanuts, or gumdrops.

Masking Tape

Rolls of masking tape are a must-have for your team challenges toolbox. Masking tape is used regularly for marking out lines and limitations and is included as a construction material for many of the tasks as well.

Possible substitutes: When marking a limit line in an outdoor setting, chalk can replace masking tape. For use in the tasks themselves, substitute sticky dots, mailing labels, bandages, or sticky notes.

Newspaper

In abundance in most households, newspaper is a great resource. Easily rolled into tubes for building, the daily paper also makes convincing costumes and hats.

Possible substitutes: Copy paper, binder paper, butcher paper, or old magazines.

Paper

Before *Team Challenges*, your team members likely thought of paper simply as a necessary school supply. But, after a few attempts to build a tower with a flat piece of binder or copy paper, they will discover that, when rolled into a tube or folded into a triangular shape, paper becomes a great support for towers or bridges. Paper can also be used to span a distance, to draw a plan, or as part of a costume.

Possible substitutes: Magazine pages, envelopes, newspaper, recycled greeting cards, or index cards.

Paper Clips

Paper clips are used extensively in team challenges. Their versatility makes them great for connectors, hooks, and hangers. By using paper clips in conjunction with a stack of drinking straws, teams can create some amazing structures. Paper clips are also great for poking holes and work well as an axle when straightened.

Possible substitutes: Hairpins or binder clips.

Paper Cups

Paper cups are most often included for the purpose of holding something. While any kind of cup will work, paper cups are the best choice, because plastic cups are difficult to poke holes through without cracking and adhesives will not stick to waxed cups.

Possible substitutes: Cardboard tubes (teams will have to invent a bottom), small cardboard boxes, zip top plastic bags, or egg cartons.

Raisins

This is another snack item claimed in the name of creative construction. Use raisins as sticky connectors, artistic details, or weights.

Possible substitutes: Miniature marshmallows, sticky dots, or gumdrops.

Rubber Bands

Every kid knows how to send a rubber band sailing across the room. It's exactly this attribute that makes rubber bands great for launching items or setting an invention in motion. Rubber bands also work as connectors.

Possible substitutes: Elastic, string, miniature bungee cords, or ponytail holders.

Spaghetti

Skip the angel-hair pasta; it's great for a meal, but it's a bit too flimsy for team challenges. You'll want to use the thicker spaghetti noodles, which work well as tower supports or to span a distance. They also work for adding length and height.

Possible substitutes: Straws, pipe cleaners, Popsicle sticks, or pretzel sticks.

Sticky Dots and Mailing Labels

Common office supplies, sticky dots and mailing labels come in a variety of shapes and sizes; all but the smallest will work. Use these to connect materials or as decorations that serve as a final touch.

Possible substitutes: Tape, sticky notes, raisins, bandages, or marshmallows.

String

Lengths of string work well for tying inventions together and can be used to hang or pull items. Avoid coated string—it is difficult to make a knot with.

Possible substitutes: Yarn, zip ties, twist ties from bread packaging, or ribbon.

Toothpicks

Toothpicks are easy to come by and easy to use, so keep a couple of boxes on hand. But don't go too cheap on these: spring for round toothpicks, as they are sturdier and will hold up better under construction circumstances than their flimsier counterparts. Toothpicks work well as short supports or connectors between items such as marshmallows or raisins, and they can even be used to hold paper together in a pinch.

Possible substitutes: Spaghetti noodles, Popsicle sticks, straws, or paper clips.

Weights

Many of the tasks you'll find in chapter 6 require teams to build structures that will hold weight. A variety of items are specified for use as weights: rubber erasers, marbles, and paper clips top the list. When looking for alternatives to use instead, keep in mind the size and type of structure your team has been asked to build.

Possible substitutes: Dry beans, sticks of gum, nails, pencils, pennies, or corks.

Yardsticks and Rulers

Used regularly by team leaders for measuring and laying out the task site, on occasion kids will also find these items on their construction materials list—either for measuring their structures or for use in creating a solution.

Possible substitutes: Tape measure or a wooden dowel.

Scrap-Box Scramble

After each task, you'll find that there are always a few items that didn't get used in the solution or are used but salvageable. Collect these materials after each team challenge and save them until you have a substantial amount of leftover items. When you have enough items, challenge your group to a scrap-box scramble. Simply place all of the materials on a suitable work surface and give the team five minutes to create something from the list below and one minute to test or present the solution:

- A tower as tall as possible
- A bridge that will hold weights
- A tower that will hold as many weights as possible
- A costume for a new football mascot
- An advertisement for a new hair care product
- A vehicle that will move at least 3 feet (0.9 m) across the floor
- A device that will fly as far as possible
- A skit depicting an unnatural disaster
- An award presentation
- A new game

4

Tiny Tasks

Warm Up with These Quick Activities

Before your team members delve into the full-blown team challenges that you'll find in later chapters, they may benefit from some simpler activities as an introduction to creative problem solving. Tiny Tasks are a great way to introduce teams and their leaders to the concept of team challenges without all of the decision making that comes along with the longer lists of materials you'll find with most of the activities. Tiny Tasks require no more than two different types of materials, eliminating many of the questions about how to use the materials to solve the problem. With Tiny Tasks, it's more a matter of learning to work together toward a common goal than seeking the most creative solution.

For example, one of the Tiny Tasks is simply to create an object out of one sheet of paper that will fly at least 10 feet (3 m). It's likely that the team will immediately come up with the idea to create a paper airplane. But what kind of paper airplane? What design is the best for distance? Who will get to do the folding? There are a number of issues that will come up just within this simple task that the team will need to address in order to succeed.

To present a Tiny Task to teams, first choose one option from the materials list for that task. Place the material(s) for the task on the table, along with a pair of scissors. Kids can use the scissors in the process of solving the challenge, but they may not use them as part of the solution. Explain the challenge to the team, set a stopwatch for two minutes, and let your team get to work!

Build a structure as tall as possible using one of the following options:

22 miniature marshmallows

16 drinking straws

5 sheets of paper and 1 roll of masking tape

24 ice cubes

5 marshmallows and 10 drinking straws

8 empty plastic water bottles

1 sheet of sticky dots and 20 toothpicks

1 box of paper clips

17 recycled bottle caps and 10 miniature marshmallows

1 cardboard tube and 10 toothpicks

1 old magazine and 1 sheet of mailing labels

10 magazine subscription cards

5 paper clips and 5 drinking straws

Create a bridge that will span 18 inches (46 cm) using one of the following options:

1 index card and 5 sticky dots

4 drinking straws

10 toothpicks and 10 marshmallows

1 file folder and 1 roll of masking tape

1 magazine and 1 roll of masking tape

3 sticky notes and 10 cotton balls

2 sheets of paper and 1 roll of masking tape

3 spaghetti noodles and 1 index card

3 bandages and 1 index card

4 paper cups and 5 drinking straws

1 cardboard tube and 3 sticky dots

1 zip top plastic bag and 10 pieces of dried spaghetti

10 rubber bands

10 Styrofoam peanuts and 10 paper clips

10 paper clips and 15 toothpicks

1 sheet of newspaper

20 toothpicks and 20 miniature marshmallows

1 Styrofoam tray and 10 paper clips

1 sheet of paper and 10 toothpicks

1 12-in. (30-cm) square of aluminum foil

Propel a ping-pong ball at least 2 feet (61 cm)—hands off!—using one of the following options:

3 rubber bands

1 18-in. (46-cm) piece of string

1 paper clip

1 sheet of newspaper

1 drinking straw

Team Tip

Stabilize the ping-pong ball by setting it on a water bottle lid.

Create a continuous, unbroken line as long as possible using one of the following options:

3 cotton balls

20 paper clips

1 strawberry basket

1 sheet of paper

1 index card

1 envelope and 5 recycled bottle caps

3 rubber bands and 3 drinking straws

1 pad of sticky notes

1 12-in. (30-cm) square of aluminum foil

3 drinking straws and 2 cotton balls

6 balloons and 3 bandages

Team Tip

Each team must use one paper clip and one yardstick in addition to the selected material(s).

Suspend a paper cup at least 6 inches (15 cm) below a yardstick (spanning two desks) using one of the following options:

1 rubber band and 1 drinking straw

3 marshmallows and 2 spaghetti noodles

3 sticky dots and 2 spaghetti noodles

1 sheet of newspaper

2 corks and 4 paper clips

7 paper clips

2 rubber bands and 4 paper clips

1 envelope

1 sheet of paper and 2 sticky dots

3 sticky dots and 1 business card

1 4-in. (10-cm) length of string and 3 paper clips

5 sticky notes

Create an object that will fly at least 10 feet (3 m) using one of the following options:

1 business card and 1 rubber band

1 drinking straw and 1 index card

1 paper cup and 1 rubber band

1 paper plate

1 sheet of newspaper and 1 paper clip

1 sheet of mailing labels and 5 spaghetti noodles

10 paper clips and 3 drinking straws

1 drinking straw and 1 paper towel

1 12-in. (30-cm) length of string and 3 paper clips

1 drinking straw and 1 sheet of mailing labels

5 cotton balls and 3 paper clips

1 sheet of paper

5

Talk It Up

Discuss Options, Share Ideas, and Make Connections

Before your team members delve into the fun and challenging tasks of structure building or the wacky world of improv, it will help if they get comfortable with one another. The activities included in this chapter are great warm-ups. The simple act of working as a group to come up with as many answers as possible to some simple questions will get their creative juices flowing, plus it will instill a feeling of camaraderie early on in each session.

By "talking it up," teammates will learn more about one another. Whether it is the knowledge that a participant has seven cats or the discovery that one teammate would choose broccoli over candy, a keener understanding of each participant's personality will make working as a team easier for all involved. Even longtime teammates may be surprised to learn something new about the members of their group after participating in some of the discussions and games suggested here.

The thought-provoking activities in this chapter will encourage participants to be creative and to explore unexpected possibilities. Some of the tasks are an introduction to brainstorming, while others require participants to practice clear communication and observation skills. Most of the activities in this chapter take only two minutes, making them a great way to start a session and give the team a jump start on feeling creative. Many of the tasks in this chapter are portable; that is, they require nothing in the way of materials, making them great to take along on outings and long drives or to fill a short time slot in your day.

As with all of the tasks in this book, these activities are about stretching the way participants think: creative answers are the most important issue here. In fact, while future chapters offer a Team Tally for recording the team's successes, scoring in this chapter is essentially nonexistent. In some activities, teammates will try to come up with as many responses as possible, but in others, they will simply work together toward a creative solution.

Once your team members have had a chance to warm up with a verbal exercise or two, they'll be relaxed and ready to take on some of the more involved tasks that entail creating structures, bridges, or costumes. But be prepared: while the activities in this chapter help warm up mental muscles, they very often lead to fits of giggles!

Getting to Know You

The Name Game

Materials

Index cards, 1 for each team member

1 marker or felt-tipped pen

1 roll of masking tape

Set Up

Write each team member's name on an index card. Shuffle the cards face down and then tape one name to each participant's back. Read the team instructions out loud.

Team Instructions

You each have a teammate's name taped to your back. The object is to correctly guess the name on your own back—but, be careful! You may not ask about the name on *your* back; you may only tell your teammates about the person whose name is on *their* backs. You may not say the person's name, gesture, point, or discuss the clothing or accessories that the teammate is wearing. When you think you are ready, give the judge your best guess. You are each limited to two guesses. If a player makes two incorrect guesses, he or she is out of the game.

Candy? Dandy!

Materials

    1 bowl
    1 bag of small candies
    Small cups, 1 for each team member

Set Up

Put the candy in the bowl. Give each team member an empty cup and seat the team in a circle. Pass the bowl of candy around the circle and ask each participant to choose some candy to put in his or her cup. Instruct the participants not to eat the candy yet. Read the team instructions out loud.

Team Instructions

For every candy that you have in your cup, you must tell one thing about yourself. You may eat the candy, one piece at a time, as you share something about yourself.

Team Tip

If some members of your team are familiar with this type of game and purposefully limit themselves to only a few pieces of candy, try this: once all the team members have filled their cups, ask participants to pass their cup in a clockwise direction to the person next to them.

People Bingo

Materials

Grids from the following pages, 1 for each team member

Set Up

Following this page are several bingo-style grids. Copy enough grids for your entire group; each participant should have one sheet. You can use the same sheet for all members or, for a more difficult challenge, make copies of all three and pass out a variety. Read the team instructions out loud.

Team Instructions

You each have a bingo-style grid to work with. Your task is to find someone in the room who fits the description given in the squares on your paper. When you find a teammate who fits the description, ask him or her to sign in the appropriate square. Participants may sign each card up to three times, but team members may not sign more than one square at a time. Your goal is to complete five squares in a row.

Has green eyes	Is an only child	Has a pet other than a dog or cat	Likes broccoli	Has his/her own e-mail address
Has a coin in his/her pocket	Is wearing sandals	Has curly hair	Is missing a tooth	Likes to read
Can recite the alphabet backward	Has read a Nancy Drew book	Has been on a motorcycle	Collects stamps	Lives in a blue house
Rides the bus to school	Is a vegetarian	Doesn't like chocolate	Knows how to ski	Plays an instrument
Plays an instrument	Doesn't have any chores	Has a tree swing	Is on a sports team	Has been on a train

Collects coins	Is the youngest child	Was born in another state	Likes lemonade	Has brown hair
Has a cat	Is wearing black shoes	Has brown eyes	Has or had braces	Can name the title of a Roald Dahl book
Has been on an airplane	Belongs to a club	Has slept on a waterbed	Doesn't have a middle name	Grows a garden at home
Has a swimming pool	Plays piano	Has been to a state capitol	Subscribes to a magazine	Has been to the ocean
Has hair long enough for a ponytail	Collects baseball cards	Has broken a bone	Can count to ten in a language other than English	Has been in a taxi

Wears glasses	Has only sisters	Doesn't own any pets	Likes apples	Has a relative that lives in another state
Has been to another country	Plays an instrument	Has never been to an ocean	Lives in a two-story house	Likes math
Has broken a bone	Wears a helmet when riding bikes	Owns a skateboard	Collects coins	Lives in a blue house
Doesn't have a middle name	Has been to a state capitol	Doesn't like chocolate	Knows how to ski	Has a garden at home
Is wearing socks other than white	Belongs to a club	Has a tree swing	Is on a sports team	Has or had braces

Fun and Games

Guess Again

Materials

1 oddly shaped or unusual item to pass around the circle

Paper and pen to tally the number of answers

Set Up

Arrange the participants in a circle. Be prepared to give the mystery item to a team member after you read the team instructions out loud.

Team Instructions

This is a verbal challenge—thinking creatively is required! You will pass an item around the circle. Each team member must answer in turn. Team members may pass on their turn only one time. You have two minutes to come up with as many answers as possible to this question: What could this item be used for?

> **Team Tip**
>
> *Potential items for this challenge are all around you. Household items such as potato mashers or hair clips are great, but so are those odd-looking items of unknown origin that you can pick up at flea markets or antique stores. Keep your eyes open for unique possibilities. With each new item that is passed around the circle, this game offers a new opportunity to think creatively.*

Circle Talk

Materials

2 slips of paper

1 marker or felt-tipped pen

Story prompts from the list that follows

Set Up

Write a start prompt and an end prompt from the list that follows on two separate slips of paper. Seat the team in a circle. Give one team member the slip of paper with the starting sentence. The person sitting to the left of the starting point should get the ending sentence. Ask the two players to read their lines out loud to the rest of the group. It is important that the participants understand who will begin and end the story and what the two sentences are. Then, read the team instructions out loud.

Team Tip

In addition to the slips of paper, you may wish to write the beginning and ending sentences on a chalkboard for the whole team to see, to help them keep track of where the story is heading.

Team Instructions

Moving from Point A to Point B is a simple concept. But when given two totally unrelated sentences, can you turn them into a cohesive story? To succeed at this task, you must think quickly. You will have a sentence to start with as well as a totally unrelated ending sentence. The first person will say the beginning sentence and, moving around the circle twice, you will each add a sentence to the story. Your story must end with the final team member reading the ending sentence.

Team Tip

Since the team must complete the circuit twice, it does them no good to reach the conclusion in just a few turns. After a few attempts, they'll learn that they must help one another to reach a successful conclusion. If your team is made up of just a few kids, you may want to increase the number of circuits the team must make to reach the end sentence.

Start: It looks like it's going to rain today.
End: I left my basketball on the bus.

Start: My computer crashed and I lost all of my games.
End: Hey, it tastes like chicken!

Start: When we went to the zoo, we saw a lemur.
End: I will survive!

Start: I'm going to the store. Do you need anything?
End: And then he did the chicken dance!

Start: Put me in coach!
End: It was Cinderella's glass slipper.

Start: On my birthday . . .
End: I've got my groove back.

Start: The dog ate my homework.
End: And the cow jumped over the moon.

Start: I've missed three days of school.
End: Finally, I can have something to eat!

Start: We traveled by car for most of the trip.
End: The book fell open to page 5.

Start: Please fill out this form.
End: Cancel my subscription.

Start: You are the winner!
End: It only takes one time.

Start: That box needs to be unpacked.

End: It's unlikely that it will rain today.

Survival Time

Set Up

This activity requires only imagination. Read the team instructions out loud. You may also want to provide photocopies of the list that follows.

Team Instructions

You and your teammates have been traveling together for weeks when you find yourselves approaching a mountaintop. The area is remote, and there are no homes or structures nearby. The weather takes a bad turn, and snow begins to fall. You are dressed lightly and find yourselves getting cold. After much discussion, you decide to continue up the mountain, taking a direct route to the nearest town. You expect that it will take at least five days to reach civilization. You have an assortment of provisions, but the rugged trip means you'll need to choose only seven items to take with you. You must choose from the items in the list that follows (sets of items may not be divided). As a team, discuss the merits of each item and the ease with which the items can be transported, and then decide which items to take with you.

1 bag of charcoal

12 unopened bottles of water

1 two-person tent

1 bucket

1 flashlight, with unknown battery life

1 flare gun with 6 flares

3 cans of chili

1 briefcase, filled with paper, 3 pens, 1 calculator, 1
    tube of lipstick, and 1 small handheld mirror

1 dozen eggs

1 lighter

1 camera bag with 3 rolls of film, lens cleaner, and 1
    35-mm camera

8 candy bars

1 bag of 5 blankets

1 double-wide sleeping bag

10 pairs of wool socks

1 Swiss army knife

1 shovel

1 ax

12 rolls of toilet paper

1 compass

1 wagon

1 1-lb (0.5-kg) box of oats

1 pair of pruning shears

It's a Draw!

Materials

Large sheets of paper

1 easel

Markers

Examples and photographs from the list that follows

Set Up

Have the team choose one person to act as team artist and then provide him or her with markers. Assemble the remaining team members and ask them to choose one of the items from the list that follows, without letting the artist know what it is. Hang a large sheet of paper on the easel in such a way that the team will not be able to watch as the artist draws. Read the team instructions out loud.

A postage stamp

A dollar bill

The logo of the local pro sports team

An example of your state's license plate

The school logo

A nickel

A key

Team Instructions

One of your teammates has been chosen to act as the team artist. The rest of you have selected a common item and will provide instructions to the artist, explaining in detail how to draw the item without telling the artist what the item is. The artist may not ask any questions and must not add any detail without direct instruction from the team. Clear instructions are essential if the artist is to create a recognizable version of the item you describe.

Team Tip

It's not as easy as it sounds! For example, given a dollar bill, the team may instruct the artist to draw a rectangle. But should it be drawn horizontally or vertically? Without that one simple piece of information, the end result will vary substantially from the actual dollar bill. This activity helps kids learn to be very precise when giving directions.

Treasure Hunting

Materials (Box #1)

1 box

1 empty water bottle

1 cotton ball

1 old floppy disk

1 paper cup

1 marble

1 rubber eraser

1 roll of masking tape

Materials (Box #2)

1 box

1 empty water bottle

1 cotton ball

1 old floppy disk

1 paper cup

1 marble

1 rubber eraser

1 roll of masking tape

1 battery

1 golf ball

1 envelope

1 rubber ball

1 sheet of sticky dots

1 compact disc

1 sock

1 cardboard tube

1 film canister

Set Up

Place the items from each list of materials in a different box and ask the team to choose one player to give directions. Situate this player apart from the team and screened from view, along with the boxful of materials from list number one. The rest of the team will have the boxful of materials from list number two to work with. Read the team instructions out loud.

Team Instructions

Clear communication is an important part of successful teamwork. In this task, you will have the opportunity to practice your communication skills. One of your teammates has a boxful of materials that is hidden from view. He or she will choose an item and describe it for the rest of the team, using only three descriptive words. This team member may not use the name or purpose of the item in the description. Once you hear the description, your task is to choose the same item from your box of materials. Both the team and the player giving the description should set the items on the table in a row as they are chosen. At the end of the task, you'll compare items to see how well you did. As you will quickly find out, it's not as easy as it seems!

Fairy-tale Fun

Set Up

Get your group giggling with some fairy-tale fun. Choose a question from the list below. Gather a pencil, a piece of paper, and a stopwatch for scoring. Read the team instructions and a fairy-tale question aloud to your group. Begin tallying their answers as soon as the team begins. There's no need to write down individual responses—just keep track of how many answers the team comes up with, so that next time they can aim for a higher count.

Team Instructions

We all have a favorite fairy-tale. But imagine what might happen if you put a twist on some famous fairy-tales and their characters. In this challenge, you have two minutes to come up with some creative answers to some silly questions. When time starts, shout out as many answers as you can think of.

Alternatives:

- Ask the team to work their way around a circle, with teammates answering in turn. You can allow team members to pass on their turn if you'd like or require that they wait for each person to come up with an answer before moving on.
- Add an improv element to the challenge, and ask the teammates to perform their answer rather than just say it aloud.

What job would Cinderella hold if she left the castle, prince-less?

If you were Humpty Dumpty, what real-life person would you call to put the pieces back together again?

Sleeping Beauty awakes from her slumber. What manufacturers want her to be their new spokesperson?

What was Rip Van Winkle most surprised by when he awoke?

If Shrek left the swamp and moved to a big city, where would he live?

What would the Three Blind Mice say if they suddenly regained their sight?

What would have happened if Old Mother Hubbard's cupboard had been full?

Jack-Be-Nimble's days of candle jumping are over. What job would be good for him?

Just how much is that doggie in the window, and why is he still for sale?

Signs of the Times

Set Up

This is a simple verbal challenge. Below are numerous combinations of three letters that you might spot on road signs, along with potential answers, to get your team started. Read the team instructions aloud and then choose one of the Signs of the Times challenges to present to your team. The three letters included in each task are random. Stretch the possibilities repeatedly by changing the three letters.

Team Instructions

Travel any road or highway and you'll see countless signs. But have you ever seen a sign that left you scratching your head in wonder? Here's your chance to come up with some clever interpretations of your own. In this challenge, you'll be given a made-up sign that might be seen along a roadside, for example, Wanted: CFD. It is your job to come up with as many potential answers as possible. In this example, CFD could stand for Clean Fill Dirt. Now, it's your turn.

Wanted: RDA

What could it mean? (Red Delicious Apples)

Found: BSM

What could it mean? (Black Spaniel, Male)

Stop at the Dewdrop Inn for some LMP

What could it mean? (Lemon Meringue Pie)

Lost: KPT

What could it mean? (Kid's Pet Turtle)

Visit RGC for the thrill of a lifetime!

What could it mean? (Radical Go-Carts)

PLU coming soon!

What could it mean? (Paradise Lost, Ukuleles)

For sale: MPR

What could it mean? (Mini Pink Rabbit)

Save the world from GGP!

What could it mean? (Greedy Gross Polluters)

Free TDB

What could it mean? (Trick Dirt Bike)

Welcome to SVL!

What could it mean? (Sierra View Lane)

Get your GSW now!

What could it mean? (Giant Seedless Watermelon)

Join us for GPT Saturday night!

What could it mean? (Ground-Pork Tacos)

Sale! 20% off RLP

What could it mean? (Rare Lincoln Penny)

RFG—Where all your dreams come true!

What could it mean? (Romantic French Getaway)

Get your HWC now!

What could it mean? (Help with Chores)

Team Talk

Learning to voice creative ideas can sometimes be difficult, since kids worry about the reactions of their peers. These simple verbal activities encourage kids to come up with a wide variety of possible answers in a short amount of time, making it not only acceptable to share unique ideas, but also desirable. Your team members will quickly learn that, in order to beat their own high score, they'll need to think of some pretty outrageous answers.

Set Up

Choose a team talk challenge from the following list. Gather a pencil, a piece of paper, and a stopwatch for scoring. Read the team instructions and a team talk challenge aloud to your group. Begin tallying their answers as soon as they begin. There's no need to write down individual responses—just keep track of how many answers the team comes up with, so that next time they can aim for a higher count. Allow the team two minutes to come up with as many answers as possible.

Team Instructions

Here's your chance to think quickly and creatively. In this challenge, you'll be asked to name different things or list as many items as possible that fit within a certain category. Once you hear the team talk challenge, you'll have two minutes to come up with as many clever answers as possible.

Team Tip

Along with many of the prompts you'll find here, I've included some examples of possible answers. Should you share the examples with your team? If you feel that the participants would benefit from hearing one or more of the examples, by all means, share them. Kids who have never done this type of activity before will likely benefit from hearing some examples early on, until they grasp the concept of an uncommon answer. If you feel that the team members can come up with creative answers on their own, let them give it a try without hearing the examples. I've been successful letting kids come up with their own answers, but then sharing a few answers of my own once they've completed the task.

Name things that can be stacked (odds, blocks, pancakes)

Name things that line up (kids, planets, racehorses)

Name things that come in a rainbow of colors (tropical fish, snow cones, yarn)

Name things that are ordered (days, weeks, a meal)

Name kinds of space (outer space, space for rent, space heater)

Name things that you lick (lollipop, an opponent, envelope)

List ways to travel (airplane, traveling light, in basketball)

Name things that flow (water, a speech, a poem)

Name things that are double (agents, photos, dares)

Name things that come in sticks (matches, gum, figures)

Name kinds of cards (greeting cards, playing cards, card sharks)

Name things that you fold (clothes, origami, poker hand)

Name things that that are numbered (chapters, trains, athletes)

Name things that you can ride (subway, bike, horse)

Name things that change or are changed (seasons, clothes, minds)

Name some dynamic duos (Batman and Robin, Calvin and Hobbes, Beauty and the Beast)

Name things that you weigh (options, fruit, yourself)

Name things that strike or are struck (matches, picketers, clocks)

Name different kinds of rocks (rock and roll, rock salt, rock-a-bye baby)

Name things that can't be undone (the passage of time, death, spoken words)

Name things that fall (night, Humpty Dumpty, leaves)

Name things that are hard (rock, tests, wood)

Name things that can break (an egg, a leg, a newsbreak)

Name things that are rolled (a ball, pennies, oats)

Name things that you can see through (a window, a lie, a telescope)

Name things that bubble (gum, soap, paint)

Name things that you keep off (the grass, mosquitoes, rain with an umbrella)

Name containers that could be used to carry liquids (a bottle, a bucket, a coconut)

Name things that are mixed (cake mix, emotions, forests)

Name things that float (a boat, corks, helium)

Name things that you can see through (glasses, windows, phony people)

Name things that are bright (headlights, smart people, smiles)

Besides salad, name what else salad tongs could be used for (picking something up, giant eyebrow tweezers)

Come up with a list of mottos (Hakuna Matata, *E Pluribus Unum*, All for One and One for All!)

Name things that come in pairs (shoes, dice, doves)

Name things that are colored orange (an orange, a Cincinnati Bengals football helmet, a safety cone)

Name things that rise and fall (elevators, empires, chests)

"Good bye" is a common way to end a conversation. What are other ways? (*Adios*, so long, *au revoir*)

Name things that can be changed (your mind, clothes, direction)

Name things that twirl (majorettes, ballerinas, tornadoes)

Name things that are timed (recipes, races, tests)

Name things that spin (tops, records, the earth)

Name things that you carry on your back (a backpack, a baby, a monkey)

Name things that you take out (garbage, Chinese food, an opponent)

List things that are printed (newspapers, the alphabet, T-shirts)

CD stands for "compact disc." What else could it stand for? (calendar day, card deck, crash-test dummy)

Name kinds of showers or use the word *shower* in a phrase (bridal, rain, April showers bring May flowers)

Come up with a list of famous dogs. Lassie is one; what are others? (Benji, Clifford, McGruff)

Name things that transform (caterpillars, Superman, seeds)

Name things that you roll (balls, toilet paper, burritos)

Name things that are tinted (windows, frosting, hair)

Name things that bounce (balls, Tigger, dryer sheets)

Name things that are spiked (hair, golf shoes, a football)

Name things that are framed (photographs, innocent victims, glasses)

Name things that ring (bells, telephones, freedom)

Name things that shine (the sun, eyes, a knight in shining armor)

Name things that flash (lights, eyes, jewelry)

Name things that are long (long johns, long and winding road, long jump)

Name things that can be stressed (points, people, bridges)

Name things that swivel (chairs, hips, fishing lures)

Name things that are linked (chains, friends, arms)

Name things that have legs (tables, people, mannequins)

Authors write books. What else can be written? (poems, advertisements, your name in the sand)

Name things that fold or are folded (chairs, poker hands, greeting cards)

Name things that are changed (diapers, tires, minds)

Name things that bend (the rules, people, roads)

Name things that fly (birds, airplanes, ideas)

Name things that glow (fireflies, brides, street signs)

Name things that close (minds, stores, eyes)

Name things that open (doors, eyes, window of opportunity)

Why might foggy weather be desirable? (it's a great backdrop for a scary movie, a cloud could hide easily, you won't need to water your garden)

Name things that snap (twigs, fingers, tempers)

Name things that are filled (bottles, gas tanks, teeth)

Name things that run (motors, kids, noses)

Name things that pop (knuckles, balloons, the weasel)

Questions and Answers

Set Up

Backward questions encourage kids to think creatively. When responding to the challenges that follow, they can't just shout out an answer; they have to rearrange their thought process and phrase their answer as a question. Figuring out what question fits the answer takes some ingenuity. Gather a pencil, a piece of paper, and a stopwatch for scoring. Read the team instructions and an answer from the following list aloud to your group. Begin tallying their answers as soon as they begin. There's no need to write down individual responses—just keep track of how many answers the team comes up with, so that next time they can aim for a higher count.

Team Instructions

Questions are usually followed by answers. In this challenge, the tables are turned. You'll be given an answer first; your task is to come up with questions that suit the given answer.

For example: The answer is cheese pizza. What is the question? Just think of all of the unique questions that fit with this answer:

> What is my favorite dinner?
> What could be used as a tire if it were overcooked?
> What can be round or square?
> What wasn't served at the first Thanksgiving?
> What is covered with melted cheese?
> What is baked, not fried?

You have two minutes to come up with as many questions as possible.

> The answer is books. What is the question?
> The answer is Bugs Bunny. What is the question?
> The answer is Lights! Camera! Action! What is the question?

The answer is a chocolate chip cookie. What is the question?

The answer is one dozen. What is the question?

The answer is Sneezy. What is the question?

The answer is microscopic evidence. What is the question?

The answer is ribbons and bows. What is the question?

The answer is sharks. What is the question?

The answer is petunia. What is the question?

The answer is medicine. What is the question?

The answer is one gallon. What is the question?

The answer is late. What is the question?

The answer is an envelope. What is the question?

The answer is a photo shoot. What is the question?

The answer is corn on the cob. What is the question?

The answer is hot air. What is the question?

The answer is flushed. What is the question?

The answer is cooperation. What is the question?

The answer is unbelievable. What is the question?

The answer is pen and paper. What is the question?

The answer is Manhattan. What is the question?

The answer is big apple. What is the question?

The answer is stormy. What is the question?

The answer is past due. What is the question?

The answer is my dog. What is the question?

The answer is location, location, location. What is the question?

The answer is the hokey pokey. What is the question?

The answer is it's a mystery. What is the question?

The answer is a blueberry. What is the question?

The answer is the library. What is the question?

The answer is rubber boots. What is the question?

The answer is cheese pizza. What is the question?

The answer is spring water. What is the question?

The answer is bigfoot. What is the question?

The answer is once a year. What is the question?

The answer is unbelievable. What is the question?

The answer is you've got mail. What is the question?

The answer is pieces of eight. What is the question?

The answer is double dribble. What is the question?

The answer is an insider view. What is the question?

The answer is travel and leisure. What is the question?

The answer is a high rise. What is the question?

The answer is speed bumps. What is the question?

The answer is X-rays. What is the question?

The answer is Jacob's ladder. What is the question?

The answer is a satellite dish. What is the question?

The answer is imagination. What is the question?

The answer is hopeless. What is the question?

The answer is the horizon. What is the question?

The answer is a merry-go-round. What is the question?

The answer is a jackrabbit. What is the question?

The answer is a train station. What is the question?

The answer is the Mad Hatter. What is the question?

The answer is a yardstick. What is the question?

The answer is the Pacific Ocean. What is the question?

The answer is the Milky Way. What is the question?

The answer is a fire truck. What is the question?

The answer is a honeycomb. What is the question?

The answer is Simple Simon. What is the question?

The answer is a celebration. What is the question?

The answer is craters. What is the question?

The answer is a diagram. What is the question?

The answer is koala bears. What is the question?

The answer is European. What is the question?

The answer is the Great Wall of China. What is the question?

The answer is snickers. What is the question?

The answer is firewood. What is the question?

The answer is nectar. What is the question?

The answer is snow skis. What is the question?

The answer is broken bones. What is the question?

The answer is peanut butter. What is the question?

The answer is bouncing. What is the question?

The answer is fast. What is the question?

The answer is orange. What is the question?

The answer is here. What is the question?

The answer is gas. What is the question?

The answer is groovy. What is the question?

The answer is ice cream. What is the question?

The answer is one-by-one. What is the question?

The answer is fire. What is the question?

The answer is dairy. What is the question?

The answer is the king. What is the question?

The answer is a pool. What is the question?

The answer is fried. What is the question?

The answer is noodles. What is the question?

The answer is history. What is the question?

The answer is common sense. What is the question?

Make the Connection

Set Up

Conservationist John Muir wrote, "When we try to pick out anything by itself, we find it hitched to everything else in the Universe." This is your team's chance to make a connection between two seemingly unrelated items. Gather a pencil, a piece of paper, and a stopwatch for scoring. Read the team instructions and a Make the Connection challenge from the following list aloud to your group. Begin tallying their answers as soon as they begin. There's no need to write down individual responses—just keep track of how many answers the team comes up with, so that next time they can aim for a higher count.

Team Instructions

Given two seemingly unrelated items, can you make a connection between them? For example, a number of possibilities arise when asked to make a connection between grass and a book:

You can use a blade of grass as a bookmark.
You can lie on the grass to read a book.
A green book cover would match the color of the grass.
You need light to read a book and grass needs light to grow.

You have two minutes to come up with as many connections as possible between the following items:

Make a connection between a game and a telephone
Make a connection between a pencil and a plan
Make a connection between a sign and a tree
Make a connection between an award and a television
Make a connection between a box and a camera
Make a connection between a straw and a cow
Make a connection between a potato and a shoe
Make a connection between a mouse and a chicken
Make a connection between a calendar and a car
Make a connection between a tent and a coffeepot
Make a connection between a tree and electricity
Make a connection between snoring and a concert
Make a connection between a map and an apple
Make a connection between a balloon and a homework
    assignment
Make a connection between a computer and a quill
Make a connection between a duck and a tomato
Make a connection between a pinecone and an arrow
Make a connection between a light bulb and a carrot
Make a connection between a vote and a beach

Make a connection between a book and shoes

Make a connection between a circus and a bolt

Make a connection between a noodle and a pair of pants

Make a connection between power and a book

Make a connection between a pedal and a screwdriver

Make a connection between a ball and a flower

Make a connection between a peach and an ant

Make a connection between a peanut and a box

Make a connection between an actor and a tree

Make a connection between a paper clip and a bicycle

Make a connection between a piano and a potato

Make a connection between a chain and a mountain

Make a connection between a block and a table

Make a connection between a library and a mechanic

Make a connection between a slide and a barn

Make a connection between a glass and a towel

Make a connection between a sock and a lion

Make a connection between a banana and a skateboard

Make a connection between an elf and an ocean

Make a connection between a rug and a lamp

6

Construction for the Whole Crew

Building Towers, Bridges, Roads, and More

Construction tasks harness kids' interest in building, giving them the opportunity to create and test structures made from a variety of common household items. While cooperation and communication are a critical part of successfully solving these tasks, another crucial aspect is the knowledge of building techniques. The tasks in this chapter provide experienced and novice builders alike with the opportunity to practice their engineering skills using an assortment of materials, always within specific guidelines.

After being given instructions to make a tower from newspaper and masking tape, it won't take long for your team members to figure out that a wide base will make a sturdier structure than a skinny one. They'll learn the importance of planning ahead when given the task of creating a structure with specific requirements—it's one thing to make a tall tower, but something else entirely to build one that will hold weights. And, as with all of the tasks included in this book, these activities require kids to listen carefully and follow directions.

From flying contraptions to bridges, towers to vehicles, the tasks in this chapter invite kids to use their imagination and creativity to construct some unusual structures and devices while working on improving their communication skills and ability to work as a team. Have fun!

Towers

Build a Tower as Tall as Possible

Materials

40 magazine subscription cards

10 marshmallows

20 toothpicks

Set Up

Gather the materials and place them on a table, making certain that the team has plenty of room in which to work. Read the list of construction materials and the team instructions out loud.

Team Instructions

You have two minutes to build a freestanding tower as tall as possible, using only the materials provided. You will be notified when you have only thirty seconds remaining. You will receive two bonus points for every inch (2.5 cm) of height.

Team Tally

	1	2	3	4	5	6	7	8	9	10
Creativity										
Communication										
Cooperation										

Bonus points: Height in inches _____ x 2 = _____

Total points: _____

Build a Tower as Light as Air

Materials

30 inflated balloons in a plastic garbage bag

1 box of bandage strips

Set Up

Gather the materials, keeping the balloons in the plastic garbage bag until needed. Place the materials in the middle of a large work area. Read the list of construction materials and the team instructions out loud.

Team Instructions

You have three minutes to build a freestanding tower as tall as possible, using only balloons and bandages. You will be notified when you have only one minute remaining. Popped balloons will not be replaced. You will receive ten bonus points if your tower exceeds a height of 3 feet (0.9 m).

Team Tally

	1	2	3	4	5	6	7	8	9	10
Creativity										
Communication										
Cooperation										

Bonus points: 10 bonus points if the tower exceeds a height of 3 feet (0.9 m)

Total points:

Create a Towering Dessert

Materials

Set Up:

1 plastic tablecloth

4 bowls

Construction:

50 pretzel sticks

10 graham crackers

10 miniature marshmallows

1 small box of raisins

1 can of whipped cream

Set Up

Cover a table with a clean plastic tablecloth. Gather the materials and put each type of food in a different bowl. Place all the materials in the center of the table. Send the team members to wash their hands, because they will want to eat their tower after it is done! Read the list of construction materials and the team instructions out loud. Note to team leader: Make sure you have extra construction materials on hand for a snack afterward.

Team Instructions

This task is going to be a treat! On the table are some edible construction materials. You may not eat any of these items until after the task is complete. Spend one minute discussing how you can create the tallest tower possible with these items. You may not touch the materials during this time. When planning time expires, you have two minutes to construct a tall tower using the materials given. You will be notified when you have only thirty seconds remaining. You will receive ten bonus points if all of the materials are used in your solution and ten bonus points if the tower exceeds a height of 12 inches (30 cm).

Team Tally

	1	2	3	4	5	6	7	8	9	10
Creativity										
Communication										
Cooperation										

Bonus points: 10 bonus points if all materials are used

Bonus points: 10 bonus points if the tower exceeds a height of 12 in. (30 cm)

Total points:

Build a Tower and Make It Collapse

Materials

Set Up:

1 roll of masking tape

1 yardstick

1 marker or felt-tipped pen

4 pieces of construction paper

Construction:

20 craft sticks

20 straws

20 toothpicks

50 miniature marshmallows

5 mailing labels

10 index cards

1 3-ft (0.9-m) length of string

Scissors*

*May not be altered

Set Up

Gather the materials and place them on a table. Mark an 18-inch (46-cm) square on the floor using masking tape. Label each side of the square with a piece of construction paper bearing a different letter, as shown in the diagram. Read the list of construction materials and the team instructions out loud.

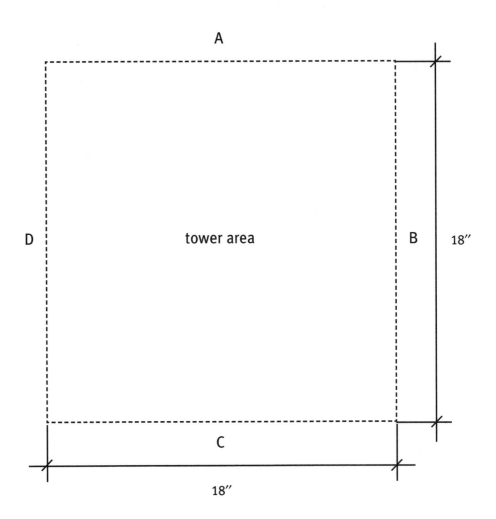

Team Instructions

You have one minute to plan and eight minutes to build a freestanding tower, using only the materials provided. You may not begin building during the one-minute planning time. The tower must be as tall as possible and built within the marked square. You will be notified when you have only one minute of building time remaining. Each side of the square is labeled with a different letter. When your tower is complete—or when time expires—you have one minute to tell the judge where the tower will collapse and to make it happen. You may not directly touch the tower after it is complete or after time expires, and its collapse must be initiated from outside the square. You will receive twenty bonus points if the tower collapses at the designated side of the square.

Team Tally

	1	2	3	4	5	6	7	8	9	10
Creativity										
Communication										
Cooperation										

Bonus points: 20 bonus points if the tower collapses according to plan

Total points:

Create a Tower from the Morning Paper

Materials

20 sheets of newspaper
1 roll of masking tape

Set Up

Gather the materials and provide ample space in which the team can work. Read the list of construction materials and the team instructions out loud.

Team Instructions

Using only the materials provided, you have five minutes to build a free-standing tower as tall as possible. You will be notified when you have only one minute remaining. You will receive five bonus points for every foot (30 cm) of height.

Team Tally

	1	2	3	4	5	6	7	8	9	10
Creativity										
Communication										
Cooperation										

Bonus points: Height in feet _____ x 5 =

Total points:

Try Your Hand at a House of Cards

Materials

1 deck of playing cards

Set Up

Locate a deck of playing cards that you no longer want. Place the cards on a sturdy tabletop. Read the team instructions out loud.

Team Instructions

Using only the playing cards on the table, you have three minutes to build a tower as tall as possible. You will be notified when you have only one minute remaining. You will receive five bonus points if your tower reaches

12 inches (30 cm) in height and twenty bonus points if it reaches 24 inches (61 cm).

Team Tally

	1	2	3	4	5	6	7	8	9	10
Creativity										
Communication										
Cooperation										

Bonus points: 5 bonus points if the tower reaches 12 in. (30 cm)

Bonus points: 20 bonus points if the tower reaches 24 in. (61 cm)

Total points:

Build a Structure as Tall as Possible

Materials

4 cardboard tubes

2 sheets of paper

10 straws

3 mailing labels

1 can of shaving cream

Set Up

Gather the materials and choose a table on which to work. You will want to protect its surface—or set the task up outside. Place all the materials on the table. Read the list of construction materials and the team instructions out loud.

Team Instructions

On the table are the materials that you can use to solve this task. You have three minutes to build a freestanding tower as tall as possible. You will be notified when you have only one minute remaining. You will receive ten bonus points if the tower exceeds a height of 18 inches (46 cm).

Team Tally

	1	2	3	4	5	6	7	8	9	10
Creativity										
Communication										
Cooperation										

Bonus points: 10 bonus points if the tower exceeds a height of 18 in. (46 cm)

Total points: _____

Tower of Two

Materials

1 old magazine

1 12-in. (30-cm) piece of masking tape

Set Up

Gather the materials and place them on a table. Read the list of construction materials and the team instructions out loud.

Team Instructions

You have three minutes to build a freestanding structure as tall as possible with only two materials: a magazine and masking tape. You will be notified when you have one minute remaining. You will receive two bonus points for every 6 inches (15 cm) of height.

Team Tally

	1	2	3	4	5	6	7	8	9	10
Creativity										
Communication										
Cooperation										

Bonus points: 2 bonus points for every 6 in. (15 cm) of height

Total points:

Fore!

Materials

    1 bag of golf tees
    20 Styrofoam trays

Set Up

Gather the materials and place them on a table. Read the list of construction materials and the team instructions out loud.

Team Instructions

On the table are some Styrofoam trays and a bagful of golf tees. You have three minutes to build a freestanding tower as tall as possible. You will be notified when you have only one minute remaining. You will receive two bonus points for every 6 inches (15 cm) of height.

Team Tally

	1	2	3	4	5	6	7	8	9	10
Creativity										
Communication										
Cooperation										

Bonus points: 2 bonus points for every 6 in. (15 cm) of height

Total points:

Build a Tower as Tall as Possible

Materials

   5 magazine subscription cards

   1 sheet of sticky dots

   25 drinking straws

   5 sheets of paper

   1 envelope

   3 cardboard tubes

Set Up

Gather the materials and place them on the floor. Provide the team with plenty of floor space in which to work. Read the list of construction materials and the team instructions out loud.

Team Instructions

You have six minutes to build a tower as tall as possible using the materials you see on the floor. You will be notified when you have only one minute remaining. You will receive ten bonus points if the tower exceeds a height of 3 feet (0.9 m).

Team Tally

	1	2	3	4	5	6	7	8	9	10
Creativity										
Communication										
Cooperation										

Bonus points: 10 bonus points if the tower exceeds a height of 3 ft (0.9 m)

Total points:

Elevate a Beach Ball

Materials

25 sheets of newspaper

1 sheet of mailing labels

1 beach ball*

*May not be altered

Set Up

Inflate a beach ball. Gather the remaining materials and provide a large area on the floor in which the team can work. Read the list of construction materials and the team instructions out loud.

Team Instructions

You have five minutes to build a structure that holds a beach ball at least 3 feet (0.9 m) above floor level. The beach ball must stay on the structure for a minimum of ten seconds. You may test the structure with the beach ball during the five-minute building period. You will be notified when you have only one minute of construction time remaining. When time expires, you must set the ball onto the structure for scoring. You will receive twenty bonus points if the ball successfully sits on top of the structure for the required amount of time.

Team Tally

	1	2	3	4	5	6	7	8	9	10
Creativity										
Communication										
Cooperation										

Bonus points: 20 bonus points if the ball sits on top of the structure for 10 seconds

Total points:

Build a Tower on Top of a Ball

Materials

Set Up:

1 beach ball

1 bowl

Construction:

1 12-in. (30-cm) square of aluminum foil

1 sheet of paper

4 pencils

4 paper clips

8 mailing labels

6 index cards

1 paper cup

Scissors*

*May not be altered

Set Up

Gather the materials. Set a beach ball in the middle of a table, on top of a bowl to prevent it from rolling around. Read the list of construction materials and the team instructions out loud.

Team Instructions

You are to build the tallest tower possible on the table, using only the given materials. But there's a catch! The tower must be constructed on top of the beach ball. The tower may not touch the tabletop or the bowl and must be sitting entirely on the ball at the completion of the task. You have one minute to make your plan, during which you may not touch the materials, and three minutes to build the tower. You will be notified when you have only one minute remaining. You will receive one bonus point for every inch (2.5 cm) of height the tower extends beyond the ball.

Team Tally

	1	2	3	4	5	6	7	8	9	10
Creativity										
Communication										
Cooperation										

Bonus points: Tower extends _____ inches beyond the ball x 1 = _____

Total points: _____

Build a Weight-Bearing Structure

Materials

10 large marshmallows

1 sheet of sticky dots

3 sheets of paper

20 toothpicks

25 straws

25 index cards

25 rubber erasers for weights*

*May not be altered

Set Up

Gather the materials and place them on a table. Read the list of construction materials and the team instructions out loud.

Team Instructions

You are to build a freestanding structure, using only the materials on the table. Your structure must be as tall as possible and be able to hold weight. You may *not* use the erasers in your solution; they are to be used as weights only. You have two minutes to think without touching the materials and four minutes to build. You will be notified when you have only one minute remaining. When building time has expired, you have two minutes to add weights—the rubber erasers—one at a time. You may continue to add

Team Tally

	1	2	3	4	5	6	7	8	9	10
Creativity										
Communication										
Cooperation										

Bonus points: Height in inches _____ x 2 = _____

Bonus points: Number of weights added to the structure without collapsing _____ x 5 = _____

Total points: _____

weights until time is up or until the tower topples (the structure must hold each new weight for at least two seconds to count). You will receive two bonus points for every inch (2.5 cm) of the completed tower's height and five bonus points for each weight added to the structure.

Bridges

Build a Bridge

Materials

Set Up:

2 chairs

Construction:

1 12-in. (30-cm) piece of masking tape

5 straws

2 index cards

15 paper clips

1 3-ft (0.9-m) length of string

Scissors*

Dry beans (for weights only)*

*May not be altered

Set Up

Gather the materials. Place two chairs together so that the seats face each other, with a 15-inch (38-cm) gap between them. Stick the length of masking tape lightly to one chair, ready for the team's use. Assemble the rest of the construction materials near the chairs. Read the list of construction materials and the team instructions out loud.

Team Instructions

You have five minutes to construct a bridge between the seats of two chairs. Your bridge must hold as many beans as possible. You may not use the scissors as part of the solution. You will be notified when you have one minute of construction time remaining. At the end of the building time, you will place the beans, one at a time, onto the bridge. You will receive one bonus point for every bean added to your bridge before the beans spill or the bridge collapses.

Team Tally

	1	2	3	4	5	6	7	8	9	10
Creativity										
Communication										
Cooperation										

Bonus points: Number of weights added to the bridge without collapsing _____ x 1 = _____

Total points: _____

Build a Long Bridge

Materials

Set Up:

2 bricks

1 yardstick

Construction:

2 12-in. (30-cm) lengths of string

15 paper clips

4 drinking straws

1 sheet of sticky dots

1 sheet of paper

5 corks

20 toothpicks

5 pieces of dried spaghetti

4 index cards

10 miniature marshmallows (for weights only)

Set Up

Gather the materials. Place two bricks on a large table along with the construction materials. Read the list of construction materials and the team instructions out loud.

Team Instructions

Your task is to build a bridge with the longest possible span. The two bricks on the table will serve as bridge towers and may be moved to any position you choose. Your bridge may not touch the table between the bricks. Distance will be measured between the bricks. You have four minutes to build the longest bridge possible. You will be notified when you have only one minute remaining. At the end of the building time, you will place the marshmallows on the bridge. Your bridge must hold all of the marshmallows on its deck in order to qualify for a bonus score. If all ten marshmallows sit on the bridge, the judge will measure the length of your bridge. You will receive one bonus point for every inch (2.5 cm) of your bridge's length.

Team Tally

	1	2	3	4	5	6	7	8	9	10
Creativity										
Communication										
Cooperation										

Bonus points: Length in inches _____ x 1 = _____

Total points: _____

A Bridge of Strength

Materials

> 1 sturdy cardboard box, about 15 in. (38 cm) square
>
> 1 bag of miniature marshmallows
>
> 1 box of toothpicks
>
> 1 box of paper clips (for weights only)

Set Up

Gather the materials. Prepare the cardboard box for the task by removing any flaps and making certain that the top of the box is entirely open. Place all the materials on a tabletop along with the box. Read the list of construction materials and the team instructions out loud.

Team Instructions

Using only the toothpicks and marshmallows, you have five minutes to build a bridge that spans from one side of the box to another. You will be notified when you have one minute remaining. Upon completion, you will have one minute to add paper clip weights to your creation. You will receive one bonus point for every weight added to the bridge before it collapses or before time runs out.

Team Tally

	1	2	3	4	5	6	7	8	9	10
Creativity										
Communication										
Cooperation										

Bonus points: Number of weights added without collapsing _____ x 1 = _____

Total points: _____

Build a Tower That Will Hold Weights

Materials

Set Up:

1 roll of masking tape

1 yardstick

1 copy of the list of construction materials

Construction:

4 cardboard tubes

5 pencils

5 paper clips

10 mailing labels

2 pieces of paper

1 strawberry basket

10 straws

Scissors*

25 rubber erasers for weights*

1 ruler*

*May not be altered

Set Up

Gather the materials. Place all the materials except the scissors, weights, and ruler on a table. Ten feet (3 m) away, mark a 2-foot (61-cm) square on the floor with tape, as shown in the diagram. Copy the list of construction materials and set it near the square, along with the scissors, weights, and ruler. Read the list of construction materials and the team instructions out loud.

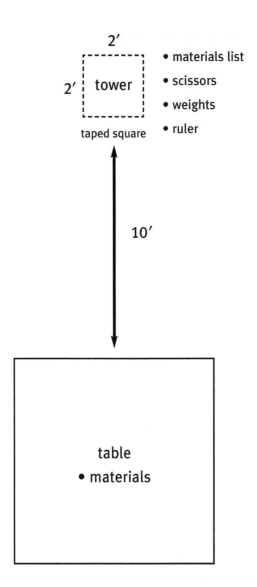

Team Instructions

Your task is to build a tower within the marked square. There is a list of materials along with a pair of scissors, weights, and a ruler near the square on the floor. These items may not be used as part of your solution. Across the room is a table full of building materials. Your team will choose a runner. Only the runner may get supplies from the table. The runner can retrieve only one item at a time and only when instructed to do so by a member of the construction crew. The construction crew may not have any more than three unused building materials near the square at any time. The tower must be at least 12 inches (30 cm) tall and should hold as many weights as possible. You will have two minutes to plan, six minutes to build, and two minutes to add weights. You will be notified when you have only one minute of building time remaining. You will receive five bonus points for every weight added to the tower before it topples. In this task, negative points will be given as well—minus one if the runner retrieves too many items or retrieves them without instruction and minus five for having more than three building materials near the square.

Team Tally

	1	2	3	4	5	6	7	8	9	10
Creativity										
Communication										
Cooperation										

Bonus points: Number of weights added without collapsing _____ x 5 =
_____

Negative points: Minus 1 for runner infractions. Minus 5 for excess building materials
_____

Total points: _____

Two Towers

Materials

Set Up:

1 roll of masking tape

1 yardstick

Construction:

1 6-in. (15-cm) cardboard tube

20 mailing labels

1 sheet of paper

10 drinking straws

5 marshmallows

6 pipe cleaners

10 pieces of dried spaghetti

3 pencils

1 box of paper clips (for weights only)

Scissors*

1 ruler*

*May not be altered

Set Up

Gather the materials. On a large table, tape off two 6-inch (15-cm) squares, 12 inches (30 cm) apart, as shown in the diagram. Place all the building materials on the table near the squares. Read the list of construction materials and the team instructions out loud.

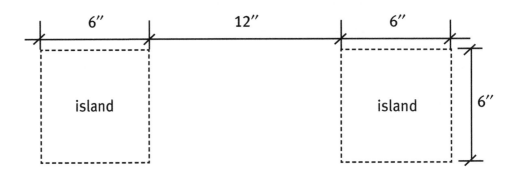

Team Instructions

The two squares you see taped on the table represent islands. Your task is to construct a bridge that spans from one island to the other without touching the table. Each tower must be made from completely different materials and stand a minimum of 8 inches (20 cm) high. All of the materials on the table may be used in building your bridge except for the paper clips—they are to be used for weights only. You have one minute to think, during which you may not touch the building materials. At the end of your one-minute thinking time, you will have eight minutes to construct your bridge.

You will be notified when you have three minutes remaining and again when you have one minute remaining. At the end of eight minutes, you will place the paper clips on the bridge, one at a time. You will receive one bonus point for each weight the bridge holds without collapsing.

Team Tally

	1	2	3	4	5	6	7	8	9	10
Creativity										
Communication										
Cooperation										

Bonus points: Number of weights added to bridge without collapsing _____ x 1 = _____

Total points: _____

Build a Bridge That Will Hold Weights

Materials

> 1 shoebox*
>
> 2 drinking straws
>
> 3 6-in. (15-cm) cardboard tubes
>
> 10 marshmallows
>
> 2 sheets of paper
>
> 10 mailing labels
>
> 10 pieces of dried spaghetti
>
> 10 toothpicks
>
> 25 rubber erasers for weights*

*May not be altered

Set Up

Gather the materials and place all but the erasers in the shoebox. Set the rubber erasers alongside the shoebox on a table. Read the list of construction materials and the team instructions out loud.

Team Instructions

In the shoebox are materials that you are to use to construct a bridge. The rubber erasers are not to be used in the solution; they are to be used for weights only. When your bridge is finished, you must be able to pass the shoebox completely under the bridge. You may not alter the shoebox in any way. Upon completion, the bridge must hold as many weights as possible. You have five minutes to build the bridge and two minutes to add weights. You will be notified when you have one minute of building time remaining. At the end of the five-minute building time, you must first demonstrate that the shoebox will pass under the bridge. You will then begin placing the weights onto the bridge. You will receive five bonus points for every weight added to the bridge before it collapses.

Team Tally

	1	2	3	4	5	6	7	8	9	10
Creativity										
Communication										
Cooperation										

Bonus points: Number of weights added without collapsing _____ x 5=

Total points:

Construct a Bridge for the Windy City

Materials

Set Up:

3 paper cups

1 yardstick

3 tennis balls

1 box

1 electric fan

Construction:

10 paper clips

2 straws

5 mailing labels

3 8-in. (20-cm) pieces of string

5 pieces of dried spaghetti

1 sheet of paper

3 rubber bands

Set Up

Gather the materials. Place three paper cups on the floor in a row, 15 inches (38 cm) apart, as shown in the diagram. Set a tennis ball on each of the cups. Put the construction materials in the box. Read the list of construction materials and the team instructions out loud.

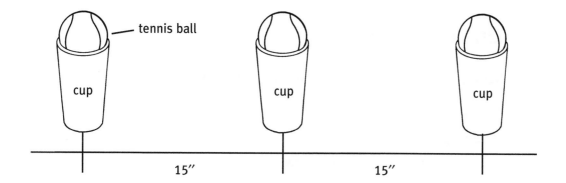

Team Instructions

On the floor are three tennis balls. Using the materials in the box, you have five minutes to build a double-span bridge from one tennis ball to the next. You may not move the tennis balls, and the bridge materials must not touch the cups or the floor. You will be notified when you have only one minute of building time remaining. When building time expires, the judge will have two minutes to test the structure's stability. You will receive ten bonus points if the bridge withstands human-generated gusts and twenty bonus points if the bridge withstands the force of an electric fan.

Team Tally

	1	2	3	4	5	6	7	8	9	10
Creativity										
Communication										
Cooperation										

Bonus points: 10 bonus points if the bridge withstands human-generated gusts

Bonus points: 20 bonus points if the bridge withstands the force of an electric fan

Total points:

Line Ups

Suspend a Line of Materials as Long as Possible

Materials

Set Up:

1 15-in. (38-cm) piece of string

1 roll of duct tape

1 box

1 stool (optional)

Construction:

1 sheet of paper

1 paper clip

5 sticky dots

10 cotton balls

10 toothpicks

1 small box of raisins

Scissors*

*May not be altered

Set Up

Gather the materials. Tie a loop at one end of the length of string. Use duct tape to securely hang the string, loop down, from the top of a doorframe. Place other materials in the box on the floor nearby. Provide a stool for the team to stand on, if necessary. Read the list of construction materials and the team instructions out loud.

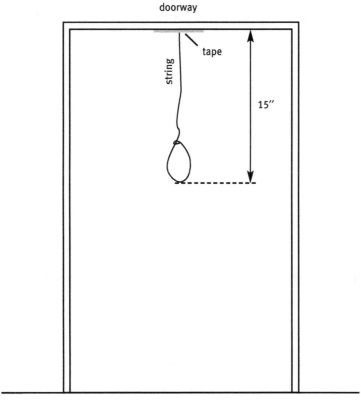

Team Instructions

You have three minutes to suspend a line of materials as long as possible from the string in the doorway. The scissors may not be used as part of the final solution. You will be notified when you have one minute remaining. You will receive fifteen bonus points if your suspended line reaches the floor.

Team Tally

	1	2	3	4	5	6	7	8	9	10
Creativity										
Communication										
Cooperation										

Bonus points: 15 bonus points if the line reaches the floor

Total points:

Variation:

To make the task more of a challenge for experienced teams, use an index card in place of the sheet of paper.

Make a Line of Materials as Long as Possible

Materials

Set Up:

5 containers (that hold the 5 following materials)

Construction:

25 miniature marshmallows

15 toothpicks

3 sheets of paper

10 straws

25 cotton balls

Set Up

Gather the materials and place each different kind of material in its own container. Set all five containers on the floor with plenty of room in which the team can work. Read the list of construction materials and the team instructions out loud.

Team Instructions

Your task is to create a line of materials as long as possible. You have five different types of materials to choose from: marshmallows, toothpicks, paper, straws, and cotton balls. You may choose only two types of materials to work with. You have one minute to discuss the materials, during which time you may not begin building. When discussion time expires, you have two minutes to construct your line. You will be notified when you have only thirty seconds remaining. Materials must be touching—no gaps allowed. You will receive one bonus point for every 12 inches (30 cm) of line. Note to team leader: The team may wish to try this task more than once, using different materials each time.

Team Tally

	1	2	3	4	5	6	7	8	9	10
Creativity										
Communication										
Cooperation										

Bonus points: Length in feet _____ x 1 = _____

Total points: _____

Create the Longest "Rope" Possible

Materials

10 large marshmallows

5 straws

15 paper clips

1 sheet of paper

10 mailing labels

3 5-in. (13-cm) lengths of string

Scissors*

1 yardstick*

*May not be altered

Set Up

Gather the materials and place them on a table near the team's work area. Read the list of construction materials and the team instructions out loud.

Team Instructions

Your task is to transform the materials on the table into a rope of sorts. The materials may be combined in any manner you choose, but the scissors may not be a part of the solution. The rope must be suspended above floor level for scoring, although it can be constructed on the floor. You have two minutes to formulate a plan without touching the materials and three minutes to construct the rope. You will be notified when you have only one minute of construction time remaining. One team member will hold each end of the finished rope for measurement, but no part of the team member will be measured. The rope may not touch the floor during measurement. The yardstick is to be used for measuring only and may not be a part of your solution. You will receive ten bonus points if the rope stays together once lifted from the floor and three bonus points for every foot (30 cm) of length. (If the rope breaks, the team may choose the longest portion remaining to be measured.)

Team Tally

	1	2	3	4	5	6	7	8	9	10
Creativity										
Communication										
Cooperation										

Bonus points: 10 bonus points if the rope stays together when lifted

Length in feet _____ x 3 =

Total points:

Line 'Em Up

Materials

1 spaghetti noodle

1 12-in. (30-cm) piece of string

1 sheet of paper

1 index card

6 sticky dots

3 ping-pong balls*

Scissors*

*May not be altered

Set Up

Gather the materials and provide the team with plenty of space to make their line on the floor—it could end up 20 feet (6 m) long. Read the list of construction materials and the team instructions out loud.

Team Instructions

Your task is to create a line on the floor using the materials provided. Your line must be made of consecutively touching materials—no gaps allowed. The scissors may not be included in your solution. You have one minute to think about and discuss the problem without touching the materials and three minutes to construct a line. You will be notified when you have only one minute remaining. You will receive five bonus points for every full foot (30 cm) of length.

Team Tally

	1	2	3	4	5	6	7	8	9	10
Creativity										
Communication										
Cooperation										

Bonus points: Length in feet _____ x 5 =

Total points:

Create a Perpendicular Line

Materials

Set Up:

1 roll of masking tape

Construction:

3 cardboard tubes

10 pieces of dried spaghetti

10 sheets of newspaper

10 paper cups

10 recycled plastic lids

5 sticky dots

1 yardstick*

*May not be altered

Set Up

Gather the materials. Tape a 10-foot (3-m) long limit line on the floor to separate the team from the building area. On one side of the line, allow at least 15 feet (4.6 m) of space for the line of materials. Allow 5 feet (1.5 m) on the opposite side of the line in which the team can work. Assemble the team and materials in the 5-foot-wide work space, as shown in the diagram. Read the list of construction materials and the team instructions out loud.

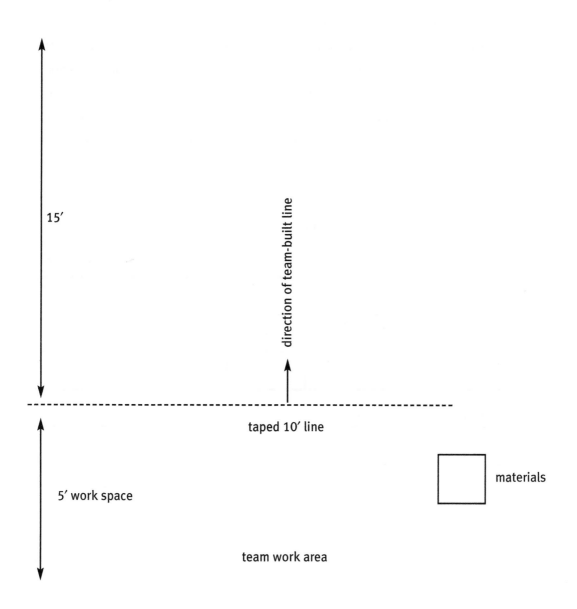

Team Instructions

In front of you is a taped line. You are to create a line of materials perpendicular to the limit line, as long as possible. The line of materials must be touching the taped line when construction time expires. The building materials must be touching—no gaps allowed. You may choose one team member to make certain that the materials are properly placed. He or she may cross the limit line to give directions and guidance but may not touch the materials or make any changes to the line. No one else is allowed to touch the floor beyond the taped line. You have two minutes to think about how to accomplish this task; you may not touch any of the materials during this time. You will then have five minutes to create your line. You may choose to restart the line, bringing all the materials back to their starting place, but no time will be added to the clock. You will be notified when you have only one minute remaining. You will receive five bonus points for every foot (30 cm) of line.

Team Tally

	1	2	3	4	5	6	7	8	9	10
Creativity										
Communication										
Cooperation										

Bonus points: Length in feet _____ x 5 = _____

Total points: _____

Waterways

Submerge a Balloon

Materials

Set Up:

1 5-gal (19 L) bucket, filled with water

1 brick

Construction:

1 6-in. (15-cm) piece of string

5 straws

1 plastic shopping bag

5 paper clips

10 mailing labels

3 binder clips*

Scissors*

1 balloon inflated to a 4-in. (10-cm) diameter*

*May not be altered

Set Up

Gather the materials. Fill the bucket with water to within 6 inches (15 cm) of the top and place a brick in the bottom of the bucket. In case of popped balloons, have several extras on hand. Assemble the materials near the bucket and provide ample room in which the team can work. Read the list of construction materials and the team instructions out loud.

Team Instructions

You are to devise a method for submerging an inflated balloon underwater. You have one minute to think without touching the materials and five minutes to build. You will be notified when you have only one minute remaining. The balloon must be submerged before the allotted time is up. The balloon must be completely submerged and remain submerged for a minimum of five seconds. You must notify the judge when you are ready for timing to begin. You will receive twenty-five bonus points if the balloon is successfully submerged.

Team Tally

	1	2	3	4	5	6	7	8	9	10
Creativity										
Communication										
Cooperation										

Bonus points: 25 bonus points if the balloon is successfully submerged

Total points:

Cushion a Water Balloon's Fall

Materials

Set Up:

1 filled water balloon

Tree branch or other tall structure outside

Construction:

1 20-in. (51-cm) piece of string

5 sheets of newspaper

10 cotton balls

1 sheet of sticky dots

1 pillowcase*

Scissors*

*May not be altered

Set Up

Gather the materials. Tie the length of string to the filled water balloon and suspend the water balloon 4 feet (1.2 m) above the ground by hanging it from a tree branch or similar tall structure outside. Assemble all the other materials nearby. Have a pair of scissors close by to cut the balloon from its string upon the expiration of the team's building time. Read the list of construction materials and the team instructions out loud.

Team Instructions

In eight minutes, the water balloon you see hanging in front of you will be severed from its lifeline and come crashing to earth. Your job is to devise a method to save the balloon. You may use the materials provided in any manner desired to prevent the water balloon from breaking. You may not alter the pillowcase or the scissors. You will be notified when you have three minutes remaining and again when you have one minute remaining. You will receive twenty bonus points if the balloon survives the fall.

Team Tally

	1	2	3	4	5	6	7	8	9	10
Creativity										
Communication										
Cooperation										

Bonus points: 20 bonus points if the balloon survives the fall

Total points:

Traverse a Tub of Water

Materials

Set Up:

1 tub, at least 3 ft (0.9 m) across, filled with water

1 roll of masking tape

1 box

Construction:

1 balloon

5 craft sticks

3 paper clips

5 corks

3 straws

5 mailing labels

2 paper cups

1 3-in. (7.6-cm) metal washer*

*May not be altered

Set Up

Fill the tub with water. On opposite sides of the tub, mark a start and fin-ish area with tape. Gather the materials in the box and place the box near the tub of water. Read the list of construction materials and the team instructions out loud.

Team Instructions

You have five minutes to devise a method to move the washer across the tub of water. The washer may not touch the bottom of the tub during its travels. When building time expires, you will have two minutes to move the washer. Your device must begin its voyage at the start area and move across the tub to the finish line. You may not touch any part of the device during its voyage across the tub. You will be notified when you have only one minute of building time remaining. You will receive twenty bonus points if the device moves the washer across the tub successfully.

Team Tally

	1	2	3	4	5	6	7	8	9	10
Creativity										
Communication										
Cooperation										

Bonus points: 20 bonus points if the device moves the washer across the tub successfully

Total points:

Float a Golf Ball

Materials

Set Up:

1 tub, at least 3 ft (0.9 m) across, filled with water

1 box

Construction:

4 corks

1 paper clip

10 toothpicks

1 plastic spoon

1 recycled plastic lid

10 Styrofoam peanuts

2 pencils

1 golf ball*

*May not be altered

Set Up

Gather the materials. Fill the tub with water. Place the other materials in the box near the tub. Read the list of construction materials and the team instructions out loud.

Team Instructions

You have five minutes to devise a method to float the golf ball across the tub of water. You will be notified when you have only one minute of building time remaining. At the end of the building time, you have two minutes to move the golf ball across the tub. You may not use the box as part of your solution. You may not touch the golf ball during its voyage across the tub. You may have only indirect contact with the flotation device during its voyage. Twenty bonus points will be awarded if the golf ball makes it successfully across the tub of water without contact from a team member.

Team Tally

	1	2	3	4	5	6	7	8	9	10
Creativity										
Communication										
Cooperation										

Bonus points: 20 bonus points for a successful voyage

Total points:

Transport Cotton Balls over Water

Materials

Set Up:

1 tub, at least 3 ft (0.9 m) across, filled with water

1 roll of masking tape

1 box

Construction:

2 corks

3 toothpicks

1 piece of paper

10 sticky dots

1 plastic yogurt container

3 straws

1 bag of cotton balls

Set Up

Fill the tub with water. On opposite sides of the tub, mark a start and finish area with tape. Place the construction materials in the box near the tub. Read the list of construction materials and the team instructions out loud.

Team Instructions

You have four minutes to develop a flotation device that will move as many cotton balls as possible from one side of the tub to another. You will be notified when you have only one minute of building time remaining. When building time expires, you will have two minutes to move the cotton balls across the water. You may not use the box as part of your solution. You may not touch the device or the cotton balls during the transportation phase. The cotton balls must remain dry; wet cotton balls are automatically disqualified. You will receive one bonus point for every dry cotton ball that is moved to the finish line.

Team Tally

	1	2	3	4	5	6	7	8	9	10
Creativity										
Communication										
Cooperation										

Bonus points: Number of dry cotton balls moved _____ x 1 = _____

Total points: _____

Build a Raft That Will Hold Weight

Materials

Set Up:

1 5-gal (19-L) bucket, filled with water

1 plastic bag

Construction:

1 recycled plastic lid, such as from a yogurt container

3 drinking straws

5 paper clips

2 un-inflated balloons

2 corks

1 6-in. (15-cm) square of aluminum foil

1 12-in. (30-cm) piece of string

50 pennies for weights*

*May not be altered

Set Up

Fill the bucket with water. Assemble the other materials in a plastic bag and place the bag in the team's work area. Read the list of construction materials and the team instructions out loud.

Team Instructions

Your task is to build a raft that will hold weight. You have four minutes to construct a seaworthy craft using only the materials provided. The raft may not be attached to the bucket in any way. You will be notified when you have one minute of construction time remaining. At the end of construction time, you will have one minute to add pennies to the raft. You will receive one bonus point for each weight the raft holds without losing any cargo. Scoring ends when the raft sinks or any pennies fall overboard.

Team Tally

	1	2	3	4	5	6	7	8	9	10
Creativity										
Communication										
Cooperation										

Bonus points: Number of pennies added to the raft _____ x 1 = _____

Total points: _____

Flights of Fancy

Create a Rocket Launcher

Materials

Set Up:

1 roll of masking tape

1 yardstick

1 box

Construction:

3 rubber bands, various sizes

2 clothespins

5 paper clips

3 Popsicle sticks

1 sheet of paper

1 index card

5 drinking straws

1 paper cup

10 miniature marshmallows

Set Up

Gather the materials. Tape a 12-inch (30-cm) square on a tabletop with masking tape. Place all the materials in the box on the table. Read the list of construction materials and the team instructions out loud.

Team Instructions

Your task is to create a rocket launcher that will fling miniature marshmallows as far as possible. Your rocket launcher must fit within the taped-off square on the table. You have five minutes to build the launcher and launch the marshmallows. The rocket launcher may be modified at any time during the five minutes. Once a marshmallow is launched, it may not be retrieved. You will be notified when you have one minute remaining. At the end of the five-minute building time—or when all marshmallows have been launched—the judge will measure the distance from the rocket launcher to the farthest-flung marshmallow. You will receive five bonus points for every foot (30 cm) the marshmallow traveled.

Team Tally

	1	2	3	4	5	6	7	8	9	10
Creativity										
Communication										
Cooperation										

Bonus points: Distance traveled by the farthest marshmallow in feet _____ x 5 = _____

Total points: _____

Make Cotton Balls Fly

Materials

Set Up:

1 roll of masking tape

1 yardstick

1 piece of colored construction paper

1 box

Construction:

1 bag of cotton balls

3 rubber bands, various sizes

2 clothespins

5 paper clips

3 Popsicle sticks

1 sheet of paper

1 index card

3 sheets of newspaper

1 sheet of sticky dots

5 drinking straws

1 paper cup

1 recycled plastic lid

1 Styrofoam tray

Set Up

Gather the materials. Mark a line on the floor using masking tape. Fifteen feet (4.6 m) away, tape a piece of colored construction paper to the floor, as shown in the diagram. Place all the materials in the box and place the box near the taped line. Read the list of construction materials and the team instructions out loud.

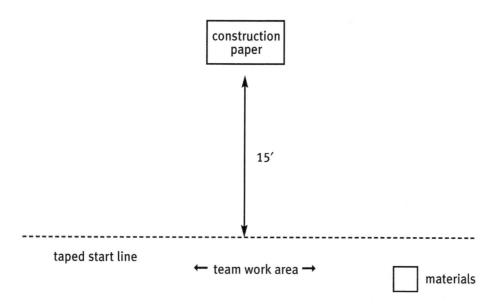

Team Instructions

Your task is to make cotton balls fly. You have five minutes to move as many cotton balls as possible from the start line and onto the square of construction paper across the room. You may not cross the taped line at any time. You will be notified when only one minute remains. You will receive one bonus point for every cotton ball on the colored construction paper when time expires.

Team Tally

	1	2	3	4	5	6	7	8	9	10
Creativity										
Communication										
Cooperation										

Bonus points: Number of cotton balls on the construction paper _____ x 1 = _____

Total points: _____

Through the Hoop

Materials

Set Up:

1 hula hoop

1 roll of masking tape

1 yardstick

Construction:

3 miniature marshmallows

1 cork

5 paper clips

1 drinking straw

1 sheet of paper

1 sheet of sticky dots

3 toothpicks

1 paper lunch sack

Set Up

Gather the materials. Hang a hula hoop from a door jamb or tree limb. This will become a target, so make sure there isn't anything nearby that can be damaged by flying objects. Tape a start line on the floor 10 feet (3 m) away from the hula hoop. Place the materials in the paper lunch sack and set the bag near the start line. Read the list of construction materials and the team instructions out loud.

Team Instructions

Your task is to create a device that will fly through the air accurately. You have four minutes to build your flight device. You will be notified when only one minute of building time remains. At the end of the building time, you will have two minutes to attempt to fly your device as many times as possible through the hula hoop. The flight must initiate from behind the start line. One team member may retrieve the device each time it is thrown. You will receive three bonus points every time your device flies through the hula hoop.

Team Tally

	1	2	3	4	5	6	7	8	9	10
Creativity										
Communication										
Cooperation										

Bonus points: Number of successful flights through the hula hoop _____ x 3 = _____

Total points: _____

Throw a Balloon

Materials

Set Up:

1 roll of masking tape

1 yardstick

Construction:

5 deflated balloons

1 rubber eraser

5 drinking straws

10 mailing labels

5 paper clips

1 paper plate

Set Up

Gather the materials and place them on a table. Mark a starting point on the floor with tape. Beyond the starting point should be a minimum of 15 feet (4.6 m) of clear space. Read the list of construction materials and the team instructions out loud.

Team Instructions

Using the materials provided, devise a method to move a balloon as far as possible from the starting point. You have five minutes to come up with a plan and test it. You will be notified when you have one minute remaining. At the end of the building time, you will have three opportunities to launch a balloon for distance. After each launch, you must decide if you want to have the distance measured or try again for a longer distance. You will receive one bonus point for every foot (30 cm) the balloon travels.

Team Tally

	1	2	3	4	5	6	7	8	9	10
Creativity										
Communication										
Cooperation										

Bonus points: Distance traveled in feet _____ x 1 = _____

Total points: _____

Invent Aircraft

Materials

  1 sheet of paper

  1 toothpick

  5 straws

  5 mailing labels

  1 envelope

  3 pipe cleaners

  1 stool (optional)

Set Up

Gather the materials and assemble them on a table. Provide plenty of space for testing aircraft. Read the list of construction materials and the team instructions out loud.

Team Instructions

Your task is to create an aircraft that will stay airborne for as long as possible. You have five minutes to build and test your aircraft. You will be notified when you have only one minute remaining. At the end of the building time, you will be allowed three launches. You may launch your aircraft from the ground or one team member may stand on a stool to initiate the launch. You will receive three bonus points for every second the aircraft is airborne. After each launch, you must make a decision: accept the score of the launch or try again for more points.

Team Tally

	1	2	3	4	5	6	7	8	9	10
Creativity										
Communication										
Cooperation										

Bonus points: Number of seconds airborne _____ x 3

Total points: _____

Moving Along

Move Ping-Pong Balls

Materials

Set Up:

1 shoebox

1 brown paper bag

4 student desks

1 yardstick

4 index cards

1 marker or felt-tipped pen

Construction:

1 12-in. (30-cm) piece of masking tape

1 12-in. (30-cm) square of aluminum foil

1 12-in. (30-cm) length of string

1 paper cup

5 paper clips

10 rubber bands

1 12-in.- (30-cm-) long cardboard tube

25 miniature marshmallows

3 sheets of paper

10 toothpicks

2 yardsticks*

10 ping-pong balls*

*May not be altered

Set Up

Place four student desks in a row, with a 2-foot (61-cm) gap between each desktop, as shown in the diagram. Place an index card on each desk, labeling the desks in numerical order. Put the ping-pong balls in the shoebox on desk number one. Gather the remaining materials and place them in the brown paper bag. Read the list of construction materials and the team instructions out loud.

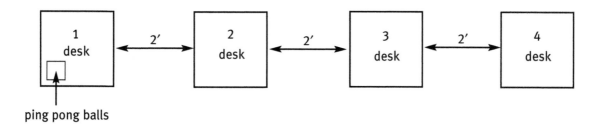

ping pong balls

Team Instructions

Your task is to move the ping-pong balls from Desk 1 to Desk 4. You may not directly touch the ping-pong balls at any time or lift the balls from one desk to another in any kind of container. Any ping-pong balls that fall to the floor are out of play. You have seven minutes to move the ping-pong balls. You will receive one bonus point for every ping-pong ball that makes it to Desk 2, three bonus points for every ping-pong ball that reaches Desk 3, and five bonus points for every ping-pong ball that reaches Desk 4.

Team Tally

	1	2	3	4	5	6	7	8	9	10
Creativity										
Communication										
Cooperation										

Bonus points: _____ ping-pong balls on Desk 2 x 1 = _____

_____ ping-pong balls on Desk 3 x 3 = _____

_____ ping-pong balls on Desk 4 x 5 = _____

Total points: _____

Invent a Vehicle

Materials

4 paper cups

6 drinking straws

1 12-in. (30-cm) square of cardboard

1 clothespin

5 mailing labels

10 rubber bands

8 sheets of newspaper

6 toothpicks*

3 cardboard tubes

20 marbles to represent hazardous waste

*May not be altered

Set Up

Gather the materials and place them on a table. Read the list of construction materials and the team instructions out loud.

Team Instructions

Your task is to develop an entirely new vehicle for transporting hazardous waste. In this task, the hazardous waste will be represented by the marbles. You have seven minutes to plan and build your invention. The toothpicks may not be altered. You will be notified when you have only one minute remaining. When construction time expires, you will have two minutes to demonstrate your vehicle to the judge by moving all of the marbles a minimum of 3 feet (0.9 m). You will receive ten bonus points if you successfully transport all of the hazardous waste.

Team Tally

	1	2	3	4	5	6	7	8	9	10
Creativity										
Communication										
Cooperation										

Bonus points: 10 bonus points if all the marbles are transported

Total points:

No-Man's Land

Materials

Set Up:

1 roll of masking tape

1 yardstick

1 brown paper bag

1 container large enough to hold 10 tennis balls

Construction:

2 un-inflated balloons

10 paper clips

1 sheet of sticky dots

10 index cards

2 paper plates

5 clothespins

5 straws

1 10-ft (3-m) length of string

10 tennis balls*

Scissors*

*May not be altered

Set Up

Gather the materials. Tape two parallel lines on the floor, 5 feet (1.5 m) apart. One is a start line, one is a finish line, and the area between the two taped lines becomes no-man's land. Place the remaining construction materials in the brown paper bag. Place the tennis balls in a separate container. Assemble the team and materials on one side of the taped area, as shown in the diagram. Read the list of construction materials and the team instructions out loud.

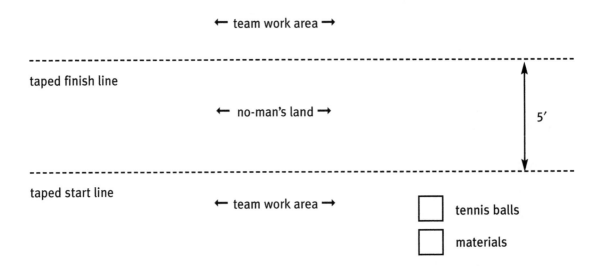

Team Instructions

Your task is to move as many tennis balls as possible from the start line to the finish line. The space between start and finish is no-man's land. You may stand on either side of no-man's land, but you may not at any time step into no-man's land. You have one minute to discuss the problem before looking into the bag of materials. You will then have six minutes to move the tennis balls across no-man's land, using your ingenuity and the materials in the bag. Balls may not be tossed, and balls that fall into no-man's land may not be retrieved. You will be notified when you have three minutes remaining and again when there is only one minute remaining. You will receive five bonus points for every tennis ball that crosses no-man's land. You will receive five negative points for every tennis balls that drops into no-man's land.

Team Tally

	1	2	3	4	5	6	7	8	9	10
Creativity										
Communication										
Cooperation										

Bonus points: 5 points for each successfully moved tennis ball

Negative points: –5 points for each tennis ball dropped in no-man's land

Total points:

Move to the Middle

Materials

Set Up:

1 roll of masking tape

1 yardstick

1 piece of colored construction paper

Construction:

1 shoebox*

1 cotton ball

1 section of a newspaper

1 paper clip

2 5-ft (1.5-m) lengths of string

1 empty plastic drink bottle

1 ping-pong ball*

*May not be altered

Set Up

Gather the construction materials and place them in the shoebox. Tape a 5-foot (1.5-m) square on the floor and tape a piece of colored construction paper in the center of the square, as shown in the diagram. Place the box of materials on the floor outside the square. Read the list of construction materials and the team instructions out loud.

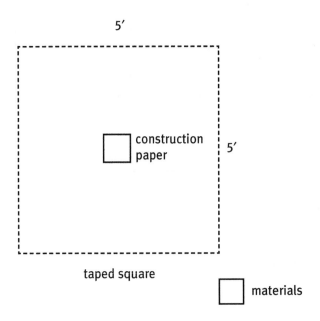

Team Instructions

For this task, you have a shoebox filled with materials. You have five minutes to move all of the materials—including the shoebox—onto the piece of construction paper you see on the floor in the middle of the square. You may not cross the taped line at any time during the completion of the task. You will be notified when you have only one minute remaining. You will receive two bonus points for every item that is touching the construction paper at the end of the five-minute time period.

Team Tally

	1	2	3	4	5	6	7	8	9	10
Creativity										
Communication										
Cooperation										

Bonus points: Number of items on the construction paper _____ x 2 = _____

Total points: _____

Move Marbles

Materials

Set Up:

1 yardstick

1 bucket

Construction:

1 roll of masking tape

5 cardboard tubes

2 sheets of paper

10 index cards

10 straws

20 toothpicks

10 marbles

Set Up

Gather the materials. Use masking tape to mark a line 12 inches (30 cm) from the edge of a table, as shown in the diagram. Place a bucket on the floor 3 feet (0.9 m) away from the taped line on the table. Read the list of construction materials and the team instructions out loud.

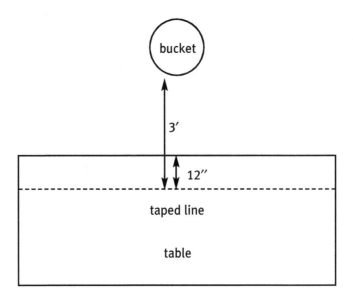

Team Instructions

You have seven minutes to create a marble maze to move marbles from the tabletop and into the bucket. Each marble must begin its movement behind the line taped on the table. Marbles may not be tossed or thrown. You will be notified when you have only one minute remaining. Once your structure is complete, you have one minute to roll marbles for points. You will receive five bonus points for every marble that reaches the bucket (with a maximum of fifty points) and five bonus points every time the marble maze successfully changes the direction in which the marble moves.

Team Tally

	1	2	3	4	5	6	7	8	9	10
Creativity										
Communication										
Cooperation										

Bonus points: Number of marbles in bucket _____ x 5 = _____

Number of times the marble changes direction on its course _____ x 5 = _____

Total points: _____

Move as Many Balls as Possible

Materials

Set Up:

1 roll of masking tape

1 yardstick

3 buckets

1 box

Construction:

2 rubber bands

3 clothespins

1 12-in. (30-cm) length of string

2 Popsicle sticks

5 index cards

2 small paper cups

10 toothpicks

5 mailing labels

25 ping-pong balls*

Scissors*

*May not be altered

Set Up

Gather the materials. Use masking tape to mark a limit line on the floor. Ten feet (3 m) away from the line, place three buckets, as shown in the diagram. Assemble the construction materials in the box and place the box near the taped line. Read the list of construction materials and the team instructions out loud.

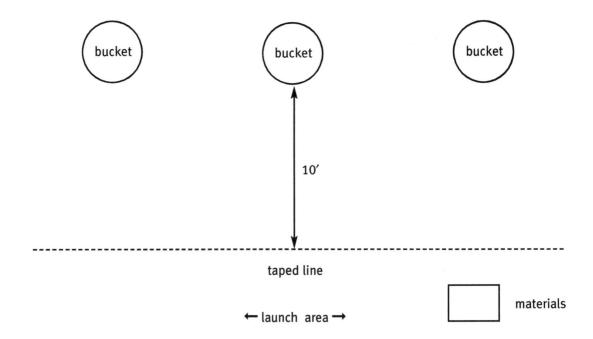

Team Instructions

You have seven minutes to build at least three ball launchers that will fire the ping-pong balls into the buckets. You will be notified when you have only one minute of building time remaining. At the end of the building time, you have three minutes to score as many points as possible. During the launching phase, neither the team nor the launchpads may cross the taped line at any time; however, you may call a cease-fire to retrieve any ping-pong balls that do not make it into a bucket. You must launch from a different device each time. One bonus point will be given for every ping-pong ball in the buckets at the end of two minutes.

Team Tally

	1	2	3	4	5	6	7	8	9	10
Creativity										
Communication										
Cooperation										

Bonus points: Number of ping-pong balls in the buckets _____ x 1 = _____

Total points: _____

Devise a Method to Move Candy

Materials

Set Up:

2 bowls

2 tables

1 large bag of candies

Construction:

10 toothpicks

1 sheet of sticky dots

2 drinking straws

1 12-in. (30-cm) length of string

5 paper clips

Set Up

Gather the materials. Pour the candies into one of the bowls and place it on a table, along with the construction materials. Place the second bowl about 10 feet (3 m) away on another table. Read the list of construction materials and the team instructions out loud.

Team Instructions

On the table are various building materials along with a bowl of candy. Your task is to move the candy from this table and into the bowl across the room. You have five minutes to develop a plan and transport the candy. Team members may not use the bowls in their solution or directly touch the candy as it is being moved. Your method must move a minimum of ten candies at once. You may move the candy at any time during the five minutes and you may alter your plan as many times as you'd like. You will be notified when you have one minute remaining. You will receive five bonus points for each successful delivery (minimum of ten candies), and the team may eat the candy that was successfully moved.

Team Tally

	1	2	3	4	5	6	7	8	9	10
Creativity										
Communication										
Cooperation										

Bonus points: Number of successful candy deliveries _____ x 5 = _____

Total points: _____

Move Cotton Balls

Materials

Set Up:

1 roll of masking tape

1 bucket

Construction:

1 yardstick

1 bag of cotton balls

6 mailing labels

3 pieces of 2-ft- (61-cm-) long string

2 spaghetti noodles

1 rubber band

1 tennis ball*

*May not be altered

Set Up

Gather the materials. Tape a 6-foot (1.8-m) square onto the floor and set a bucket in the center of the square, as shown in the diagram. Place the remaining materials outside the square. Read the list of construction materials and the team instructions out loud.

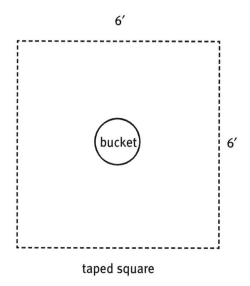

6′

6′

bucket

taped square

Team Instructions

You have one minute to discuss a system to move the cotton balls into the bucket. You may not touch any of the materials during this time. Once planning time has expired, you have four minutes to move the cotton balls into the bucket without crossing the taped line. Cotton balls may be moved into the square from any direction. You will be notified when you have only one minute remaining. You will receive one bonus point for every cotton ball in the bucket.

Team Tally

	1	2	3	4	5	6	7	8	9	10
Creativity										
Communication										
Cooperation										

Bonus points: Number of cotton balls in the bucket _____ x 1 = _____

Total points: _____

Move a Can

Materials

3 clothespins

2 paper clips

2 sheets of paper

5 mailing labels

6 straws

1 3-ft (0.9-m) length of string

1 unopened can of food, about 16 oz (470 mL)*

*May not be altered

Set Up

Gather the materials and place them on the floor, providing ample working room. Read the list of construction materials and the team instructions out loud.

Team Instructions

You have four minutes to devise a method to move the can as far as possible across the floor. The can must stay in an upright position at all times. The string may not directly touch the can and you may touch only the string during the one-minute moving period. When time expires, you will have one minute to move the can across the floor, as far as possible. You will be notified when you have only one minute of construction time remaining. You will receive three bonus points for every foot of distance the can travels.

Team Tally

	1	2	3	4	5	6	7	8	9	10
Creativity										
Communication										
Cooperation										

Bonus points: Distance traveled in feet _____ x 3 = _____

Total points: _____

Super Suspension

Devise a Method to Suspend an Egg

Materials

Set Up:

2 tables or desks

1 rubber band

1 yardstick

1 roll of masking tape

1 paper clip

Construction:

3 paper clips

1 sheet of paper

5 toothpicks

2 straws

1 index card

1 egg*

*May not be altered

Set Up

Gather the materials. Place two tables or desks about 2 feet (61 cm) apart. Slide a rubber band over a yardstick and place the yardstick so that it spans the tables, as shown in the diagram. Secure the yardstick in place with masking tape. Unbend a paper clip to form a hook and hang it from the rubber band. Place the construction materials on a table. Read the list of construction materials and the team instructions out loud.

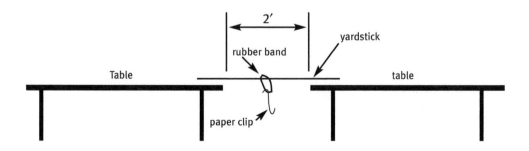

Team Instructions

Your task is to use the materials you see on the table to suspend an egg from the paper clip that is hanging from the yardstick. You have five minutes to devise a solution. The egg must be hanging from the paper clip when time expires. You will be notified when you have only one minute remaining. You will receive twenty bonus points if your egg is successfully suspended.

Team Tally

	1	2	3	4	5	6	7	8	9	10
Creativity										
Communication										
Cooperation										

Bonus points: 20 bonus points if the egg is hanging as instructed

Total points:

A Weighty Proposal

Materials

Set Up:

2 desks or tables

1 yardstick

1 roll of masking tape

Construction:

1 paper cup

3 spaghetti noodles

2 bandages

1 rubber band

2 straws

1 12-in. (30-cm) piece of string

1 cardboard tube

1 cup full of marbles (for weights only)*

1 ruler* for team to use in measuring solution

*May not be altered

Set Up

Gather the materials. Place two desks or tables 2 1/2 feet (0.8 m) apart. Set a yardstick so that it spans the distance between the desks, as shown in the diagram, and secure the yardstick in place with masking tape. Place all the construction materials on a separate table. Read the list of construction materials and the team instructions out loud.

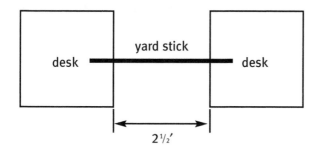

Team Instructions

Your task is to suspend a paper cup from the yardstick so that it will hold weight. You may use the materials you see on the table in constructing your solution. The marbles are to be used as weights only and may not be used in your solution. The top of the cup must hang at least 1 foot (30 cm) below the yardstick, and no part of the cup or materials may touch the ground. You will have three minutes to suspend the cup. You may test your plan during this time. At the end of the three minutes, one team member will begin placing weights into the empty cup. You will earn five bonus points for each weight added to the cup. You may add as many weights as you like and determine when to stop adding weights, but if the cup spills, there will be no bonus points awarded for the weights.

Team Tally

	1	2	3	4	5	6	7	8	9	10
Creativity										
Communication										
Cooperation										

Bonus points: Number of weights added to the cup without spilling _____ x 5 = _____

Total points: _____

Suspend as Many Marshmallows in the Air as Possible

Materials

Set Up:

1 box

Construction:

1 5-ft (1.5-m) length of string

1 bag of large marshmallows

10 paper clips

5 straws

10 pieces of dried spaghetti

Set Up

Gather the materials and place them in the box. Provide an area in which the team can work. Read the list of construction materials and the team instructions out loud.

Team Instructions

You have two minutes to devise a method to hold as many marshmallows as possible above ground level. No team member is to be in direct contact with any marshmallows during the scoring process. Scoring begins at the end of the two-minute building time. You will receive one bonus point for each successfully suspended marshmallow.

Team Tally

	1	2	3	4	5	6	7	8	9	10
Creativity										
Communication										
Cooperation										

Bonus points: Number of suspended marshmallows _____ x 1 = _____

Total points: _____

Make a Piñata

Materials

Set Up:

1 3-ft (0.9-m) piece of string

1 roll of duct tape

1 bowl

1 bag of individually wrapped candies

Construction:

5 drinking straws

1 paper napkin

1 paper plate

2 sheets of paper

5 sticky dots

5 paper clips

1 bandage strip

1 ruler*

*May not be altered

Set Up

Gather the materials. Tie a loop in one end of the string. Using duct tape, securely attach the string to a doorframe with the loop hanging down, as shown in the diagram. Open the bag of candy and put the wrapped candy in a bowl, discarding the outer package. Place all the materials except for the ruler along with the candy in the work area. Read the list of construction materials and the team instructions out loud.

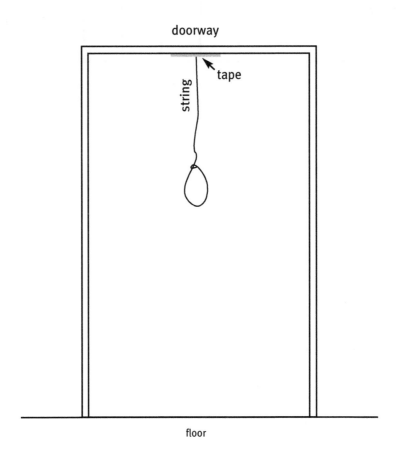

Team Instructions

You are planning a birthday party, but the piñata you ordered hasn't arrived. You must use the materials provided to create a piñata of your own. You have five minutes to build a piñata that holds all of the candy. At the end of construction time, your piñata must be hanging from the loop in the string. You will be notified when you have only one minute remaining. Upon completion, team members will have the opportunity—one at a time—to use the ruler to strike the piñata. You will receive five bonus pints for each blow that the piñata takes without breaking, up to a maximum of fifty points. At the end of the task, you may eat the candy.

Team Tally

	1	2	3	4	5	6	7	8	9	10
Creativity										
Communication										
Cooperation										

Bonus points: Number of hits without breaking _____ x 5 = _____

Total points: _____

Suspend a Paper Clip over the Edge of a Table

Materials

    5 mailing labels

    1 sheet of paper

    3 rubber bands

    3 drinking straws

    3 spaghetti noodles

    1 paper clip

    1 ruler*

*May not be altered

Set Up

Gather the materials and place them on a table. Read the list of construction materials and the team instructions out loud.

Team Instructions

Your task is to suspend the paper clip as far as possible beyond the edge of the tabletop. You have five minutes to devise and implement a plan using only the materials provided. The paper clip must be suspended before time is up. You will be notified when you have one minute remaining. You will receive two bonus points for every inch (2.5 cm) between the paper clip and the edge of the table.

Team Tally

	1	2	3	4	5	6	7	8	9	10
Creativity										
Communication										
Cooperation										

Bonus points: Length in inches _____ from the edge of the table x 2 =

Total points:

Suspend an Egg in Mid-Air

Materials

Set Up:

2 tables

1 yardstick

1 tray

Construction:

2 paper clips

1 envelope

5 drinking straws

1 sheet of paper

10 mailing labels

1 egg*

*May not be altered

Set Up

Gather the materials. Push two tables side-by-side, 18 inches (46 cm) apart. Place all the materials on one of the tables. Set a tray under the gap between the tables to ease cleanup, as shown in the diagram. Read the list of construction materials and the team instructions out loud.

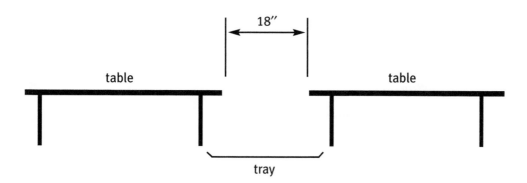

Team Instructions

With only the materials provided, you must devise a method to suspend the egg between the two tables. You have five minutes to come up with a solution. You will be notified when you have one minute remaining. At the end of the building time, the egg must be hanging without the aid of any team member. You will receive ten bonus points for an unbroken egg.

Team Tally

	1	2	3	4	5	6	7	8	9	10
Creativity										
Communication										
Cooperation										

Bonus points: 10 bonus points for an unbroken egg

Total points:

Creative Constructions

Invent a Noisemaker

Materials

Set Up:

1 roll of masking tape

1 yardstick

1 box

Construction:

2 un-inflated balloons

10 paper clips

1 sheet of sticky dots

1 rubber band

1 sheet of paper

10 index cards

2 paper plates

1 empty plastic bottle

5 clothespins

5 straws

1 5-ft (1.5-m) length of string

1 ruler*

*May not be altered

Set Up

Gather the materials. Tape an 18-inch (46-cm) square on the floor. Assemble all the materials in the box and place it near the taped square. Read the list of construction materials and the team instructions out loud.

Team Instructions

On the floor is a taped square. Your task is to build a noisemaker that makes a sound that can be heard from 15 feet (4.6 m) away. Your noisemaker must fit completely within the taped square and may not touch the floor outside of the square. Team members may not directly touch the device to generate noise; the noise must be initiated from outside of the taped square. You have seven minutes to build your noisemaker. You will be notified when you have three minutes of construction time remaining and again when you have one minute remaining. At the end of construction time, you must be ready to make some noise. You will receive ten bonus points if the noise is heard by the judge.

Team Tally

	1	2	3	4	5	6	7	8	9	10
Creativity										
Communication										
Cooperation										

Bonus points: 10 bonus points if the noise is heard by the judge

Total points:

Design Displays

Materials

Set Up:

1 box

Construction:

1 6-in. (15-cm) cardboard tube

4 drinking straws

1 sheet of paper

2 pipe cleaners

3 rubber bands

1 clothespin

3 toothpicks

4 miniature marshmallows

4 paper clips

1 binder clip

1 envelope

1 plastic spoon

1 bandage

5 raisins

10 to 15 miniature cars*

*May not be altered

Set Up

Gather the materials and place them in the box. Provide a tabletop on which the team can work. Read the list of construction materials and the team instructions out loud.

Team Instructions

Your team has been chosen to create display pedestals for a miniature car show. The cars in the box each need to sit on top of a pedestal that elevates the car a minimum of 1 inch (2.5 cm) above the tabletop. You may use the materials in the box in any combination, but you may use each type of material only once. You have four minutes to create as many different pedestals as possible. You will be notified when you have one minute remaining. You will receive five bonus points for every car sitting on a pedestal at the end of the building time.

Team Tally

	1	2	3	4	5	6	7	8	9	10
Creativity										
Communication										
Cooperation										

Bonus points: Number of cars on pedestals _____ x 5 =

Total points:

Build a Structure That Supports a Book

Materials

A stack of newspapers

1 roll of masking tape

1 heavy, hardback book*

*May not be altered

Set Up

Gather the materials and provide a workspace on the floor. Read the list of construction materials and the team instructions out loud.

Team Instructions

You have four minutes to build a structure out of newspaper and tape that will support the book. When the structure is complete, two team members must be able to clasp hands underneath it, without touching either the structure or the book. You will receive ten bonus points for a successful solution.

Team Tally

	1	2	3	4	5	6	7	8	9	10
Creativity										
Communication										
Cooperation										

Bonus points: 10 bonus points for a structure that supports the book

Total points:

Desktop Display

Materials

Set Up:

1 box

Construction:

10 spaghetti noodles

10 drinking straws

25 cotton balls

1 sheet of mailing labels

5 paper cups

3 sheets of paper

5 miscellaneous recycled items, such as berry baskets, plastic lids, etc.

Set Up

Gather the materials and place them in the box near a student desk or similarly sized table. Read the list of construction materials and the team instructions out loud.

Team Instructions

You have five minutes to build a single structure that physically touches all four edges of the desktop. You will be notified when you have one minute remaining. You will receive ten bonus points if you use every single material in your solution.

Team Tally

	1	2	3	4	5	6	7	8	9	10
Creativity										
Communication										
Cooperation										

Bonus points: 10 bonus points if every material is used

Total points:

Team Accommodations

Materials

A stack of newspapers, 6 in. (15 cm) high

1 roll of masking tape

Set Up

Gather the materials. Clear a large area in which the team can work and set the materials nearby. Read the list of construction materials and the team instructions out loud.

Team Instructions

Using only a roll of tape and a stack of newspapers, can you build a structure that will hold your entire team? You are to create a freestanding, three-dimensional structure that your whole team can get into. You have ten minutes to build your solution. You will be notified when you have three minutes remaining and again when you have one minute remaining. You will receive twenty bonus points if all of the members of your team fit into the structure.

Team Tally

	1	2	3	4	5	6	7	8	9	10
Creativity										
Communication										
Cooperation										

Bonus points: 20 bonus points if the entire team fits into the structure

Total points:

Build an Arch Tall Enough for a Team Member to Pass Under

Materials

1 small box of spaghetti noodles

1 bag of miniature marshmallows

Set Up

Clear a large area in which the team can work. Gather the materials and set them near the building area. Read the list of construction materials and the team instructions out loud.

Team Instructions

Your task is to build an arch. Your arch must be tall enough for a team member to pass under. You have two minutes to discuss a plan, without touching the materials. At the end of the discussion time, you have five minutes to build your arch. You will be notified when you have one minute of construction time remaining. At the end of the five minutes—or when your arch is complete—the judge will watch as a chosen team member passes under the arch. You will receive ten bonus points if the team member successfully passes under the arch without knocking it down.

Team Tally

	1	2	3	4	5	6	7	8	9	10
Creativity										
Communication										
Cooperation										

Bonus points: 10 bonus points if a team member passes under the arch without knocking it down

Total points:

Go the Distance

Materials

   3 craft sticks

   1 sheet of paper

   5 paper clips

   1 binder clip

   1 paper cup

   1 sheet of sticky dots

   1 12-in. (30-cm) length of string

   3 marshmallows

Set Up

Gather the materials and provide the team with a large, open area that allows for flight practice. Read the list of construction materials and the team instructions out loud.

Team Instructions

Your task is to create a flying device that travels the longest distance possible. You will have three launch opportunities, but you need to make a decision. You can make one device and fly it three times, or you can create three different devices, flying each of them once. In either case, you will receive two bonus points for every foot (30 cm) of the longest flight. You have five minutes to plan and build. You will be notified when only one minute of building time remains.

Team Tally

	1	2	3	4	5	6	7	8	9	10
Creativity										
Communication										
Cooperation										

Bonus points: Longest traveling distance in feet _____ x 2

Total points:

Build a Big Structure

Materials

3 cereal or shoeboxes

3 cardboard tubes (12 in. [30 cm] or less)

1 sheet of mailing labels

5 corks

5 pieces of paper

5 straws

5 paper clips

1 egg carton

Set Up

Gather the materials and provide a large area in which the team can work. Read the list of construction materials and the team instructions out loud.

Team Instructions

You have five minutes to build a structure that one team member can pass under. You will be notified when you have only one minute remaining. At the end of the allotted construction time, the team will choose one person to pass under the structure. The entire body of the chosen team member must pass completely under the structure in less than one minute without touching any part of the structure. If the judge announces that the structure is touched, you may try again as long as there is time remaining. You will receive twenty bonus points if the team member successfully passes under the structure.

Team Tally

	1	2	3	4	5	6	7	8	9	10
Creativity										
Communication										
Cooperation										

Bonus points: 20 bonus points if the team member successfully passes under the structure

Total points:

Spin a Marshmallow

Materials

Set Up:

1 felt-tipped pen

Construction:

1 sturdy cardboard box, 12 in. (30 cm) square

1 rubber band

3 corks

5 straws

1 box of toothpicks

1 marshmallow

10 paper clips

Set Up

Gather the materials and place them on a table. Mark a line all the way around the marshmallow with a felt-tipped pen to help count revolutions during the scoring phase. Read the list of construction materials and the team instructions out loud.

Team Instructions

With the given materials, you must create a device that will allow a marshmallow to spin. You have ten minutes to problem solve and build the structure. You will be notified when you have three minutes remaining and again when you have one minute remaining. At the end of construction time, one team member will spin the marshmallow for bonus points; no other contact is allowed. You will receive ten bonus points if the marshmallow spins for more than five revolutions.

Team Tally

	1	2	3	4	5	6	7	8	9	10
Creativity										
Communication										
Cooperation										

Bonus points: 10 bonus points for more than five revolutions

Total points: _____

Create a Miniature Amusement Park

Materials

 25 toothpicks

 25 paper clips

 5 rubber bands

 10 plastic bottle caps

 10 mailing labels

 1 12-in. (30-cm) piece of string

 1 12-in. (30-cm) square of cardboard*

*May not be altered

Set Up

Gather the materials and place them on a table. Read the list of construction materials and the team instructions out loud.

Team Instructions

You have five minutes to build an amusement park on the square of cardboard. The cardboard may not be altered. You will be notified when you have only one minute remaining. At the end of the allotted time, you will have two minutes to present your amusement park to the judge. Each team member will be expected to tell about a different aspect of the park. Five bonus points will be awarded for each separate feature built within the park.

Team Tally

	1	2	3	4	5	6	7	8	9	10
Creativity										
Communication										
Cooperation										

Bonus points: Number of attractions in the park _____ x 5 = _____

Total points: _____

Recreate a Work of Art

Materials

Set Up:

1 plastic tablecloth

Construction:

1 package of graham crackers

1 bag of pretzels

10 large marshmallows

1 can of whipped cream

1 small box of raisins

Set Up

Gather the materials. Cover a table or large work surface with a clean plastic tablecloth. Instruct team members to wash their hands. Assemble the materials on the table. Read the list of construction materials and the team instructions out loud.

Team Instructions

On the table are some edible materials. You have five minutes to use these ingredients to recreate a famous work of art. You will be notified when you have only one minute remaining. You will receive ten bonus points if your solution is recognizable as the intended work of art. Once scoring is complete, you may devour your creation.

Team Tally

	1	2	3	4	5	6	7	8	9	10
Creativity										
Communication										
Cooperation										

Bonus points: 10 bonus points if the art is recognizable

Total points:

Build a Road

Materials

1 paper towel tube

5 paper clips

3 index cards

5 mailing labels

1 paper cup

5 rubber bands

1 sheet of paper

10 toothpicks

10 straws

Scissors*

1 small toy car*

*May not be altered

Set Up

Gather the materials and place them on a table. Read the list of construction materials and the team instructions out loud.

Team Instructions

Your task is to build a road on which a toy car can travel a long distance using the materials on the table. The road that you create must allow the car to move without any contact from team members. The car may not be pushed and must move along your road without any direct team contact. You can touch the car only as it is being placed on the road. You have four minutes to build. You will be notified when you have only one minute remaining. After building time has expired, you may test-drive your creation for one minute, marking the distance that the car travels during each attempt. You will receive one bonus point per inch (2.5 cm) for the longest distance the car travels during the one-minute testing period.

Team Tally

	1	2	3	4	5	6	7	8	9	10
Creativity										
Communication										
Cooperation										

Bonus points: Longest distance the car travels in inches _____ x 1 = _____

Total points: _____

Build a Structure that Holds an Egg

Materials

Set Up:

Newspapers

1 container for the egg

Construction:

10 miniature marshmallows

10 toothpicks

25 straws

1 egg

Scissors*

*May not be altered

Set Up

Gather the materials. Cover a table with newspapers and place all the materials on the table. Put the egg in a container to prevent it from rolling around. Read the list of construction materials and the team instructions out loud.

Team Instructions

Can you build a structure that will hold an egg? Using the materials you see on the table, you must devise a method to hold one egg a minimum of 3 inches (7.6 cm) above the tabletop. You may not use the container that is holding the egg in your solution. You have two minutes to come up with a plan without touching any of the materials and three minutes to build. You will be notified when you have only thirty seconds remaining. The egg must be sitting on the structure when building time expires. You will receive ten bonus points for an elevated and unbroken egg.

Team Tally

	1	2	3	4	5	6	7	8	9	10
Creativity										
Communication										
Cooperation										

Bonus points: 10 bonus points for an elevated and unbroken egg

Total points:

Create Shapes

Materials

1 6-in. (15-cm) cardboard tube

1 sheet of paper

2 pipe cleaners

3 rubber bands

1 clothespin

3 toothpicks

2 drinking straws

1 paper clip

1 12-in. (30-cm) square of aluminum foil

1 3-in. (7.6 cm) piece of string

2 miniature marshmallows

1 crayon

3 spaghetti noodles

1 rubber eraser*

*May not be altered

Set Up

Gather the materials and place them on an empty table. Read the list of construction materials and the team instructions out loud.

Team Instructions

Use the materials provided to create as many closed shapes as possible in five minutes. Shapes are to be formed on a flat surface and must not have any visible gaps between the materials. The rubber band may not be used as a circular shape. Team members may not speak during the construction time. Materials can be altered, but scissors are unavailable. You will be notified when you have only one minute remaining. You will receive five bonus points for each different shape you create.

Team Tally

	1	2	3	4	5	6	7	8	9	10
Creativity										
Communication										
Cooperation										

Bonus points: Number of shapes created _____ x 5 = _____

Total points: _____

Build the Alphabet

Materials

    2 straws

    5 paper clips

    10 toothpicks

    1 clothespin

    1 12-in. (30-cm) square of aluminum foil

    1 12-in. (30-cm) length of string

    5 recycled plastic lids

    3 rubber bands

    Scissors*

*May not be altered

Set Up

Gather the materials and place them on an otherwise empty table. Read the list of construction materials and the team instructions out loud.

Team Instructions

Everyone is familiar with the alphabet, right? Your task today is to create the alphabet from the construction materials you see on the table. You must create as many letters as possible in five minutes. The letters must be created in alphabetical order—you can't jump ahead to easy letters. Team members may not speak during building time. You will be notified when you have only one minute remaining. You will receive one bonus point for every complete and recognizable letter.

Team Tally

	1	2	3	4	5	6	7	8	9	10
Creativity										
Communication										
Cooperation										

Bonus points: Number of letters created _____ x 1 = _____

Total points: _____

Duplicate Designs

Materials

    Sheets of paper, 1 for each team member
    Sheets of sticky dots, 1 for each team member
    Paper clips, 3 for each team member
    Toothpicks, 5 for each team member
    Paper lunch sacks, 1 for each team member

Set Up

Gather the construction materials; you'll need one complete set of materials for each participant. Place the materials in paper lunch sacks so that each player has the same exact materials to work with. Read the list of construction materials and the team instructions out loud and give each player a bag of materials.

Team Instructions

Choose a player to be the director and have that person turn his or her back to the group. The rest of the team will spread out around the room. You each have a bag of materials. Your task is to create an item with instructions from the director. When you are ready, the director will start building something with the items in his or her bag. While building, the director will explain what he or she is doing, so that the rest of the team can duplicate the creation. In this task, clear communication is essential. All of the construction materials must be used. There is no time limit for this task. When all players have finished, compare your designs and discuss the task.

Team Tally

	1	2	3	4	5	6	7	8	9	10
Creativity										
Communication										
Cooperation										

Total points:

7

Move It!

Physical Activities

Physical tasks require that teammates learn to depend upon one another. These tasks require teams to actively solve a problem that one person alone would not be capable of solving. Moving or sorting objects within specific constraints, such as using nonverbal methods of communication or being limited to the use of only one hand, teaches teammates to work closely together to achieve a common goal.

Each task in this chapter emphasizes the importance of teamwork and reminds teams that, without one another to depend upon, some of these tasks would be impossible.

Move Some Candy

Materials

1 bowl
1 bag of colored candy (such as Skittles, M&Ms, or Sweet Tarts)
Pieces of construction paper, 1 to match each color of candy
1 blindfold

Set Up

Pour the candy into the bowl. Then, ask the team to choose a candy sorter. Set the construction paper in a row on a table. Read the team instructions out loud.

Team Instructions

Your task is to sort the candies into color groups. The candy sorter must place each candy on the coordinating color of construction paper—blindfolded. You must accomplish this using a nonverbal method of communication. You have two minutes to establish a method of nonverbal communication. At the end of planning time, blindfold the candy sorter. You must now begin using your nonverbal method of communication to help your teammate place the candies on the correct pieces of paper. You have four minutes to move as much candy as possible. Once a piece of candy has been placed on a piece of construction paper, it may not be moved. You will be notified when you have only one minute remaining. You will receive one bonus point for every correctly placed piece of candy. You will receive five negative points for every use of verbal communication. Once the task is completed, you may eat the candy.

Team Tally

	1	2	3	4	5	6	7	8	9	10
Creativity										
Communication										
Cooperation										

Bonus points: Number of properly placed candies _____ x 1 = _____

Negative points: Number of speaking infractions _____ x 5 = _____

Total points: _____

Four Square

Materials

1 yardstick

1 roll of masking tape

1 bucket

4 items, one of each of the following colors: red, blue, green, and yellow

1 blindfold

Set Up

Tape a 10-foot (3-m) square on the floor. Set a bucket in the middle of the taped square, as shown in the diagram. Blindfold the player of the team's choice. Place a different colored item at each corner of the taped square. Read the team instructions out loud.

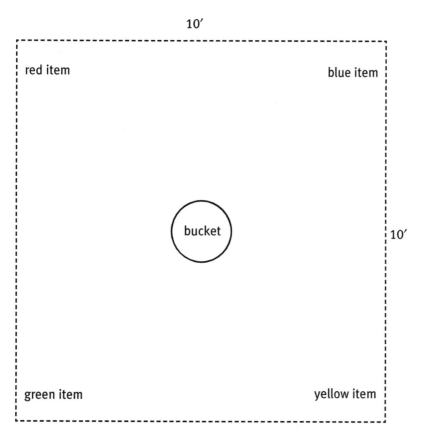

taped square

Team Instructions

There is a square taped on the floor. At each corner is an item, each one a different color. You have two minutes to work as a team to move all four of the items into the bucket in the center of the square, in this order: red, blue, green, yellow. But here's the catch: your *blindfolded* team member will move the items. As a team, you must help your teammate pick up the colored items in the appropriate order—red, blue, green, yellow—and place them into the bucket. There is another catch, though: you must choose one person to stand at each corner of the square. Each player can offer instructions to *his or her corner only*. Anyone on the team can provide instructions for reaching the bucket. You will be notified when you have only one minute remaining. You will receive five bonus points for each successfully moved item.

Team Tally

	1	2	3	4	5	6	7	8	9	10
Creativity										
Communication										
Cooperation										

Bonus points: Number of properly placed items _____ x 5 = _____

Total points: _____

Remove Your Shoes

Materials

1 2-ft (61-cm) square cardboard box

Styrofoam peanuts to fill the box

Set Up

Fill the cardboard box with Styrofoam peanuts. Have up to four team members at a time lie on their backs, with their feet together in the air to form a pedestal. Balance the box on their raised feet. Read the team instructions out loud.

Team Instructions

The box on your feet is full of Styrofoam peanuts. You must remove your shoes without spilling any of the peanuts from the box. Every team member must have at least one foot on the box at all times. There is no time limit. You will receive twenty bonus points if you succeed.

Team Tally

	1	2	3	4	5	6	7	8	9	10
Creativity										
Communication										
Cooperation										

Bonus points: 20 bonus points if all team members remove their shoes without spilling the peanuts

Total points:

Roll a Tennis Ball Through a Hole

Materials

1 large box, such as one used to hold a large appliance

1 tennis ball

1 ruler

Set Up

Cut the bottom half off of the box and discard the top half. Trim the sides of the box bottom to about 4 inches (10 cm) high, to create a shallow tray. Cut a 4-inch (10-cm) hole in the center of the box bottom. Place the tennis ball in one corner of the box. Read the team instructions out loud.

Team Instructions

You have two minutes to roll the tennis ball through the hole in the box as many times as possible. You must lift the box off the ground as a team, but you may not touch the tennis ball, except to pick it up each time it drops through the hole. You will receive five bonus points every time the ball drops through the hole.

Team Tally

	1	2	3	4	5	6	7	8	9	10
Creativity										
Communication										
Cooperation										

Bonus points: Number of times the ball drops through the hole _____ x 5 = _____

Total points: _____

Variation

Have the team attempt to complete the challenge with only one hand on the box.

Move a Rubber Ball

Materials

1 12-in. (30-cm) diameter rubber ball
1 5-gal (19-L) bucket

Set Up

Stand the team members in a circle, with their backs toward the center of the circle. Have them link arms. Place the rubber ball on the floor in the middle of the circle of kids. Set the bucket on the floor 15 feet (4.6 m) away. Read the team instructions out loud.

Team Instructions

There is a bucket across the room. You have three minutes to move the ball from its starting point and into the bucket. You may not at any time touch the ball with your hands. You will be notified when you have only one minute remaining. You will receive ten bonus points if the ball is in the bucket at the end of the three minutes.

Team Tally

	1	2	3	4	5	6	7	8	9	10
Creativity										
Communication										
Cooperation										

Bonus points: 10 bonus points if the ball is in the bucket

Total points:

Cut, Tie, Zip!

Materials

2 pieces of paper

1 pair of lace-up shoes (untied)

1 container filled with 25 toothpicks

1 sandwich-sized zip top plastic bag

Scissors*

*May not be altered

Set Up

Gather the materials and place them on a table. Read the construction materials list and team instructions out loud.

Team Instructions

You have two minutes to complete the following tasks. Cut one piece of paper into four pieces and another piece of paper into six pieces. Then, tie the shoelaces on both shoes into bows. Finally, put the toothpicks into the zip top bag and seal it. But here's the catch: each team member can only use one hand in completing this task and cannot directly touch any of the toothpicks. You will be notified when you have only one minute remaining. You will receive five bonus points for each successfully completed task.

Team Tally

	1	2	3	4	5	6	7	8	9	10
Creativity										
Communication										
Cooperation										

Bonus points: Number of tasks completed _____ x 5 = _____

Total points: _____

Lay Down a Path

Materials

Set Up:

1 roll of masking tape

1 yardstick

Construction:

1 copy of the following diagram

3 sheets red construction paper

4 sheets blue construction paper

3 sheets green construction paper

Set Up

Gather the materials. Tape two lines, 10 feet (3 m) apart, on the floor. Make a copy of the diagram. Divide the team in two, telling them that one group will be the Card Placers and the other group will be the Task Masters. Give the Card Placers the construction paper and the Task Masters the diagram. The Card Placers may not look at the diagram. Read the team instructions out loud.

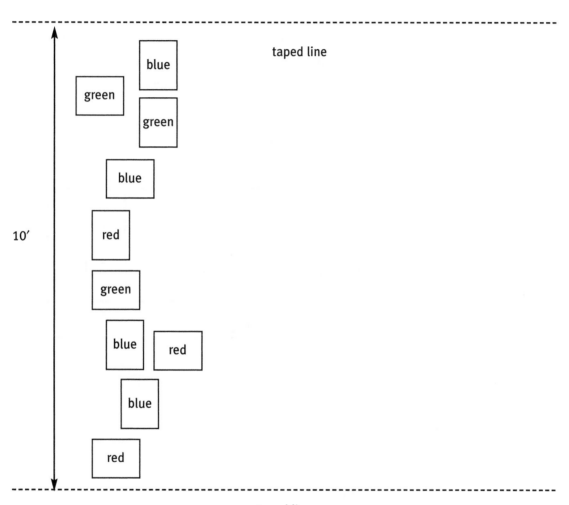

Team Instructions

Your task is to bridge the distance between the lines taped on the floor, without talking. You must create a path according to the diagram given to the Task Masters. The Task Masters will use nonverbal cues to instruct the Card Placers how and where to place the construction paper. The Card Placers may not look at the diagram at any time. You have two minutes to plan a nonverbal method of communication. When planning time expires, you must cease any verbal communication and you may not gesture. You will have five minutes to place the construction paper in the correct order to bridge the distance. Only the Card Placers may place cards. You will be notified when you have only one minute remaining. You will receive two bonus points for every correctly placed sheet of construction paper.

Team Tally

	1	2	3	4	5	6	7	8	9	10
Creativity										
Communication										
Cooperation										

Bonus points: Number of properly placed sheets of paper _____ x 2 = _____

Total points: _____

Make a Paper Chain

Materials

10 sheets of paper

2 sheets of sticky dots

Scissors*

*May not be altered

Set Up

Gather the materials and place them on a table, allowing ample room in which the team can work. Read the construction materials list and team instructions out loud.

Team Instructions

Your task is to assemble a paper chain as long as possible. The catch: each team member can use only one hand during assembly. You have four minutes to create your paper chain. You will be notified when you have one minute remaining. You will receive twenty bonus points if the chain is ten links long and three bonus points for each additional link.

Team Tally

	1	2	3	4	5	6	7	8	9	10
Creativity										
Communication										
Cooperation										

Bonus points: 20 bonus points if the chain is 10 links long _____

Number of additional links _____ x 3 = _____

Total points: _____

Elevate Balloons

Materials

Inflated balloons, 6 for each member of the team, in
large plastic garbage bags

Set Up

Put the inflated balloons in the garbage bags. Gather the team nearby. Read the team instructions out loud.

Team Instructions

Your task is to elevate as many balloons as possible above floor level. The balloons may not be set upon any surface. You have three minutes to clear the floor! You will be notified when you have one minute remaining. You will receive two bonus points for every balloon above floor level at the end of the allotted time.

Team Tally

	1	2	3	4	5	6	7	8	9	10
Creativity										
Communication										
Cooperation										

Bonus points: Number of balloons elevated _____ x 2 = _____

Total points: _____

Assemble a Paper Clip Chain

Materials

1 box of paper clips

Set Up

Gather the materials and provide ample space in which the team can work. Read the team instructions out loud.

Team Instructions

You have five minutes to make a chain of paper clips as long as possible. But there's a catch! This is a one-handed task: all team members must place one hand behind their backs. No talking is allowed during this task. You will be notified when there is one minute remaining. You will receive twenty bonus points if your chain measures at least 12 inches (30 cm) long.

Team Tally

	1	2	3	4	5	6	7	8	9	10
Creativity										
Communication										
Cooperation										

Bonus points: 20 bonus points if the chain measures at least 12 in. long

Total points:

Hit the Wall

Materials

Set Up:

1 roll of masking tape

1 yardstick

Construction:

Long cardboard tubes (such as wrapping paper tubes),
    1 for each team member

10 ping-pong balls

Set Up

Use masking tape to mark a line on the floor 6 inches (15 cm) from the face of a wall, as shown in the diagram. Fifteen feet (4.6 m) away, mark a start line on the floor with tape. Gather the construction materials and set them in a pile by the start line. Read the construction materials list and team instructions out loud.

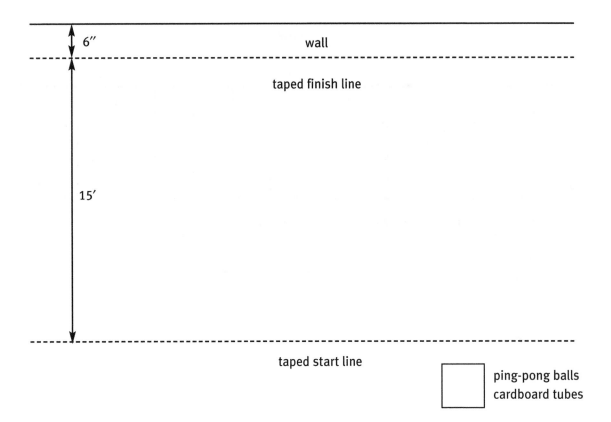

Team Instructions

You have ten ping-pong balls to move to the wall. Each ping-pong ball must cross the finish line taped near the wall. Only the cardboard tubes can touch the ping-pong balls. Each ping-pong ball that begins its journey to the wall must be in direct contact with a cardboard tube at all times. If your cardboard tube is touching the ping-pong ball, your feet may not move. You have four minutes to move all of the ping-pong balls across the finish line. You will be notified when you have one minute remaining. You will receive twenty bonus points if you successfully move all of the ping-pong balls across the line.

Team Tally

	1	2	3	4	5	6	7	8	9	10
Creativity										
Communication										
Cooperation										

Bonus points: 20 bonus points if all the balls cross the line

Total points:

Line Up in Order of Height

Materials

Blindfolds, 1 for each team member

Set Up

Provide a clear space in which the team can work. Blindfold all the teammates and tell them that no talking is allowed. Read the team instructions out loud.

Team Instructions

You have two minutes to line up in order of height, from shortest to tallest. There will be no talking during this task. You will receive twenty bonus points for a correct solution.

Team Tally

	1	2	3	4	5	6	7	8	9	10
Creativity										
Communication										
Cooperation										

Bonus points: 20 bonus points if the team successfully lines up according to height

Total points:

Move the Entire Team

Materials

    2 12-x-18 in. (30-x-46 cm) pieces of cardboard

    1 roll of duct tape

    1 roll of masking tape

    1 yardstick

Set Up

Transform the pieces of cardboard into "magic shoes," as shown in the diagram. For each shoe, fold a 20-inch (51-cm) length of duct tape in half, sticky sides together, to make a strap. Tape each end of this strap securely to the cardboard, using more duct tape. The "magic shoes" will resemble old-fashioned snowshoes. On the floor, mark two lines with masking tape approximately 12 feet (3.7 m) apart. Assemble the team members on one side of this line and give them the magic shoes. Read the team instructions out loud.

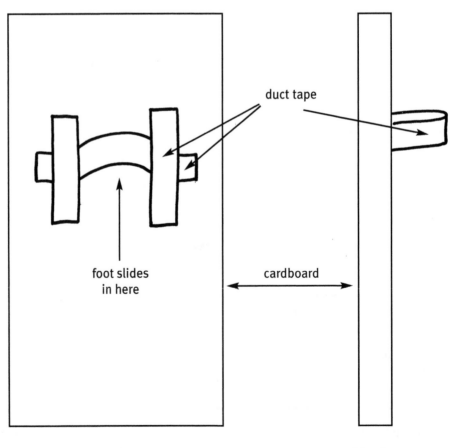

duct tape

foot slides
in here

cardboard

top view

side view

Team Instructions

Your team is stranded! You are standing at the edge of a vast river. You may not touch any part of the river, but you must move every team member across. You are lucky, though. You have at your disposal a pair of magic shoes that allows you to walk across the water. You must not drop the magic shoes in the river. If you drop the shoes in the river, your team will be forever stranded. You have eight minutes to devise and implement a plan to move your entire team across the river without making a splash. You will be notified when you have three minutes remaining and again when you have one minute remaining. You will receive five bonus points for every team member who successfully moved across the river and an additional ten bonus points if the entire team makes it across. If the magic shoes land in the river, the challenge comes to a halt and no points will be awarded.

Team Tally

	1	2	3	4	5	6	7	8	9	10
Creativity										
Communication										
Cooperation										

Bonus points: Number of team members successfully moved _____ x 5 = _____

_____ 10 bonus points if the entire team made it across _____

Total points: _____

Move as Many Balls as Possible

Materials

1 roll of masking tape

1 yardstick

1 bucketful of ping-pong balls (a minimum of 30)

1 empty bucket

1 24-in. (61-cm) square piece of cardboard

Set Up

Tape a start line on the floor. Tape a finish line on the floor about 10 feet (3 m) away, as shown in the diagram. Place the bucket of balls and the piece of cardboard at the start line and assemble the team near the bucket. Set the empty bucket across the finish line. Read the team instructions out loud.

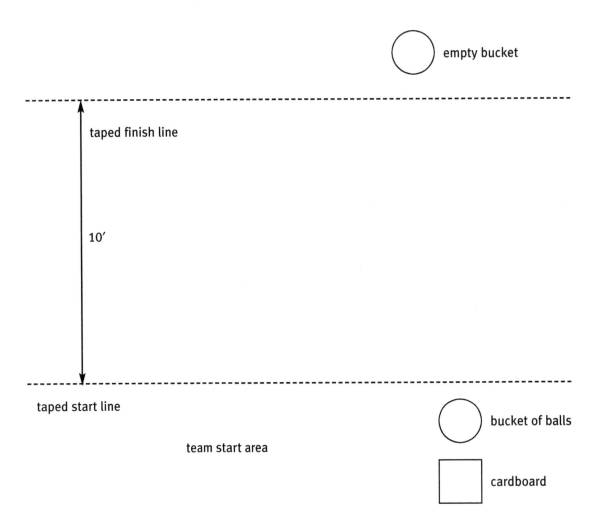

Team Instructions

Near the starting point is a bucket full of ping-pong balls and a piece of cardboard. You have five minutes to move as many balls as possible from the start line and into the bucket at the finish line. You may not bend or alter the piece of cardboard. Team members may not touch the ping-pong balls at any time while in the space between the start and finish lines. Once the balls cross the line, it's hands off! You will be notified when you have only one minute remaining. You will receive ten bonus points if you successfully deposit all of the balls into the empty bucket.

Team Tally

	1	2	3	4	5	6	7	8	9	10
Creativity										
Communication										
Cooperation										

Bonus points: 10 bonus points for moving all of the balls into the empty bucket

Total points:

Fill a Bag with Dice

Materials

1 plastic cup
10 dice
1 zip top plastic sandwich bag

Set Up

Gather the materials. Place the dice in the plastic cup. Put the plastic cup on the table along with the plastic bag. Read the team instructions out loud.

Team Instructions

On the table is a cup with ten dice in it. There is also a plastic bag. You have five minutes to move all of the dice from the cup into the plastic bag. You may not use your hands, feet, or mouth. You will be notified when you have only one minute remaining. You will earn ten bonus points if, at the end of five minutes, all of the dice are in the bag.

Team Tally

	1	2	3	4	5	6	7	8	9	10
Creativity										
Communication										
Cooperation										

Bonus points: 10 bonus points if all of the dice are moved into the bag

Total points:

Traverse an Obstacle Course

Materials

1 roll of masking tape

An assortment of items to be used as obstacles, such as
   chairs, buckets, desks, or cones

1 blindfold

Set Up

Create an obstacle course and mark a start and finish line with tape. Read the team instructions out loud. Note: During the task, you will need to monitor the blindfolded team member for safety.

Team Instructions

Choose one team member to maneuver through the obstacle course you see in front of you. (Note to team leader: You may wish to demonstrate the path at this point.) This team member will be blindfolded and totally dependant upon his or her teammates to complete the course. You have two minutes to develop a nonverbal method of communication that will guide your blindfolded teammate safely through the obstacle course. There is no time limit for successfully maneuvering the obstacle course. You will receive ten bonus points if the blindfolded team member crosses the finish line.

Team Tally

	1	2	3	4	5	6	7	8	9	10
Creativity										
Communication										
Cooperation										

Bonus points: 10 bonus points if the blindfolded teammate crosses the finish line

Total points:

Move Tennis Balls

Materials

 1 roll of masking tape

 1 yardstick

 1 bucketful of tennis balls

 1 empty bucket

Set Up

Tape a start line on the floor. Tape a finish line on the floor about 10 feet (3 m) away. Place the bucket of balls at the start line and assemble the team near the bucket. Set the empty bucket across the finish line. Read the team instructions out loud.

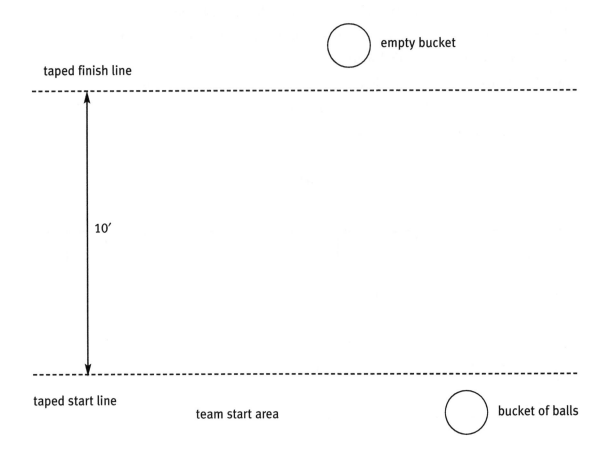

Team Instructions

Near the starting point is a bucketful of tennis balls. You have five minutes to move as many balls as possible from the full bucket into the empty bucket across the finish line. You must designate one team member who can touch the tennis balls. The chosen team member may not cross the start line at any time. The remaining team members must move the tennis balls to the finish line without touching the tennis balls with their hands or arms at any time. Team members—other than the person assigned this job—who touch a tennis ball with their hands or arms after the start time must leave the game. You will be notified when you have one minute remaining. You will receive ten bonus points if all of the tennis balls are moved from the start bucket to the finish bucket in the allotted time.

Team Tally

	1	2	3	4	5	6	7	8	9	10
Creativity										
Communication										
Cooperation										

Bonus points: 10 bonus points if all of the tennis balls are moved to the finish bucket

Total points:

Have a Seat

Set Up

Clear a large space in which the team can work and arrange the chairs. Read the team instructions out loud.

Team Instructions

Working as a team means that you can depend upon one another. In this task, you must figure out how to give each other a break. Without touching anything in the room other than the floor, figure out a way that every team member can sit on a teammate's lap. You have one minute to discuss your ideas. At the end of one minute, all verbal discussion must cease. You have three minutes to make your plan work. You can notify the judge that you have successfully completed the task at any time during the three minutes. Ten bonus points if you succeed.

Team Tally

	1	2	3	4	5	6	7	8	9	10
Creativity										
Communication										
Cooperation										

Bonus points: 10 bonus points if every team member sits on another's lap

Total points:

Move Paper

Materials

100 pieces of 1-in.- (2.5-cm-) square paper
Drinking straws, 1 for each team member
1 large bowl

Set Up

Gather the materials and place the bowl in the center of a table. Scatter the pieces of paper on the table around the bowl. Provide each team member with a straw. Read the team instructions out loud.

Team Instructions

You have three minutes to move all of the pieces of paper from the table-top and into the bowl. You may use only the straws to move the paper. You may not touch the paper with any part of your body. You will be notified when you have one minute remaining. You will receive twenty-five bonus points if you move every piece of paper into the bowl.

Team Tally

	1	2	3	4	5	6	7	8	9	10
Creativity										
Communication										
Cooperation										

Bonus points: 25 bonus points if all pieces of paper are in the bowl

Total points:

Make a Picture Using Cotton Balls

Materials

1 full bag of cotton balls
1 blindfold

Set Up

Gather the materials and provide a clear tabletop on which to work. Place the cotton balls on the table. Read the team instructions out loud.

Team Instructions

Your task is to create a picture using only cotton balls. You have one minute to discuss a plan and choose one person to be the artist. At the end of the planning time, blindfold the artist. The team then has four minutes to direct the artist in creating a picture on the tabletop. You will be notified when you have one minute remaining. At the end of four minutes, the artist will remove the blindfold and give a thirty-second presentation to the judge explaining the picture. The rest of the group must remain silent during the presentation.

Team Tally

	1	2	3	4	5	6	7	8	9	10
Creativity										
Communication										
Cooperation										

Total points:

Pile Bean Bags

Materials

    1 roll of masking tape

    1 yardstick

    25 beanbags

Set Up

Gather the materials. Tape two lines on the floor 12 feet (3.7 m) apart. Place the beanbags behind one of the lines and assemble the team nearby. On the opposite side of the taped-off area, mark an "X" with tape, as shown in the diagram. Read the team instructions out loud.

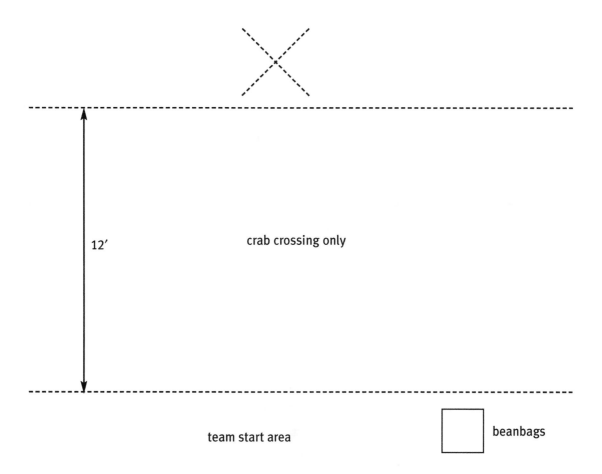

12′

crab crossing only

team start area

beanbags

Team Instructions

There is a taped-off area on the floor. This area is reserved for crab cross-ing only. Your task is to build a pile of beanbags on the far side of the taped-off area, on the "X." You must move the beanbags from the starting point, across the taped-off area and onto the "X." The only method you may use for crossing the taped-off area is the crab walk. You have three minutes to move all of the beanbags. You will receive twenty bonus points if all of the beanbags are physically touching in a pile.

Team Tally

	1	2	3	4	5	6	7	8	9	10
Creativity										
Communication										
Cooperation										

Bonus points: 20 bonus points if all of the beanbags are touching in a pile

Total points: _____

Line Up!

Materials

Index cards, 1 for each participant

Blindfolds, 1 for each participant

1 marker or felt-tipped pen

Set Up

Write a letter on each index card; depending on the difficulty desired, you can use letters in exact order (a, b, c, and d) or you can use a random pattern (for example, a, g, k, and s). Just make certain that there are no duplicate letters. Give each team member an index card with instructions to keep the letter a secret. Now, blindfold the players. Read the team instructions out loud.

Team Instructions

You were each assigned a letter of the alphabet and were all then blindfolded. Your task is to arrange yourselves in alphabetical order without speaking.

There is no time limit. When you are satisfied with your positions, you must announce that you are done. You will receive ten bonus points if you successfully complete the task.

Team Tally

	1	2	3	4	5	6	7	8	9	10
Creativity										
Communication										
Cooperation										

Bonus points: 10 bonus points if the team lines up correctly

Total points:

Create a Shape

Materials

1 20-ft (6-m) length of heavy string, ends tied together to form a loop

1 marker or felt-tipped pen

Index cards

1 container for the index cards

Blindfolds, 1 for each team member (optional)

Set Up

Draw a variety of closed shapes on the index cards. Place the cards in a container. Ask each group member to hold onto the string, standing in a circle. Choose one player to draw an index card out of the container. Read the team instructions out loud.

Team Instructions

Your teammate picked a card from a container. Pass the card around the circle, making certain that everyone on the team has a chance to study the shape drawn on the card. Your task is to create the shape shown on the index card with the string, with your eyes closed. Players may not let go of the string at any time. Teammates must come to an agreement about when the shape is complete before opening their eyes to observe.

Variation

Try it with team members facing away from the center of the circle or with only one hand on the string.

Team Tally

	1	2	3	4	5	6	7	8	9	10
Creativity										
Communication										
Cooperation										

Total points:

Move the Entire Team

Materials

  1 roll of masking tape
  1 yardstick
  Beach balls, 1 per team member

Set Up

Mark a finish line on the floor using tape. Line up team members parallel to the finish line and about 20 feet (6 m) away. Place beach balls between players' hips and instruct them not to drop the balls. Read the team instructions out loud.

Team Instructions

Have you ever heard the term *joined at the hip*? In this task, you have the opportunity to see exactly what that means. Without dropping any of the beach balls, you have three minutes to work your way to the finish line. If you drop a beach ball, you must begin again at the start line. You will be notified when you have one minute remaining. You will receive ten bonus points if you successfully complete the challenge.

Variation

Try it with tennis balls, ping-pong balls, or balloons.

Team Tally

	1	2	3	4	5	6	7	8	9	10
Creativity										
Communication										
Cooperation										

Bonus points: 10 bonus points if the team successfully crosses the finish line

Total points:

Move It on Over

Materials

1 round, flannel-backed vinyl tablecloth

Set Up

Direct team members to lie on their backs in a circle, feet toward the center of the circle and in the air. Drape the tablecloth, vinyl side up, over the team's raised feet. Read the team instructions out loud.

Team Instructions

The tablecloth resting on your feet has two sides: a fuzzy side and a smooth side. Currently, the smooth side of the tablecloth is facing up. Working together, your task is to flip the tablecloth completely over, using only your feet, so that the fuzzy side of the tablecloth is facing up. You have five minutes in which to complete this task. If the tablecloth falls from your feet, the judge will place it back on your feet in the original starting position (smooth side up). You will be notified when you have one minute remaining. You will receive ten bonus points if you successfully flip the tablecloth over.

Team Tally

	1	2	3	4	5	6	7	8	9	10
Creativity										
Communication										
Cooperation										

Bonus points: 10 bonus points if the tablecloth is flipped over

Total points:

Move Goo

Materials

2 cups (460 mL) cornstarch

About 2 cups (460 mL) water

1 plastic mixing bowl

1 edged cookie sheet

1 plastic measuring cup, 4-cup (1 L) capacity

Set Up

Blend the cornstarch and water in the bowl, adding the water a little at a time until the mixture begins to feel thick. To test the mixture, try scooping some up and rolling it into a ball; let go to see if the mixture flows from your hand. If it doesn't hold together under pressure, add a bit more cornstarch. If it doesn't flow, add more water. Now, pour the goo onto the cookie sheet and place it on a table outside. Fifteen feet (4.6 m) away, place the measuring cup on another table. Assemble the team near the cookie sheet full of goo. Read the team instructions out loud.

Team Tip

You will likely have goo everywhere by the time this task is complete. Not to worry: it cleans up easily if you simply hose off your work area. Any goo on clothing will brush off once it dries, but if you'd like, you can offer the team smocks or old T-shirts to wear.

Team Instructions

On the table is a bunch of goo. Your task is to move the goo from this table and into the measuring cup on the other table. You will have one minute to discuss a plan and experiment with the mixture, but you may not use this time to move any goo. You will have two minutes to move as much goo as possible from here to the measuring cup. All hands must be out of the goo and empty when it's time to begin moving goo. You will be notified when you have thirty seconds remaining. You will receive five bonus points for every one-fourth cup (60 mL) of goo in the measuring cup at the end of two minutes.

Team Tip

Mixing the cornstarch and water together creates a non-Newtonian liquid. The combination will hold together and appear to be a solid under pressure but will act like liquid without direct pressure.

Team Tally

	1	2	3	4	5	6	7	8	9	10
Creativity										
Communication										
Cooperation										

Bonus points: Number of one-fourths of a cup of goo in the measuring cup _____ x 5 =

Total points:

Line Up

Materials

Index cards, 1 per team member

1 marker or felt-tipped pen

24-in. (61-cm) lengths of string, 1 per team member

1 hole punch

Set Up

Number several index cards in sequence. Punch a hole in each card and tie a string through the hole, necklace style. Assemble the team shoulder-to-shoulder in a line and hang the cards on each player so that the card hangs down their backs. Read the team instructions out loud.

Variation

For a more difficult challenge, number the cards using only odd or even numbers.

Team Instructions

You each have a numbered card hanging on your back. During this task, you will be able to see everyone's card but your own. Your task is to assemble yourselves in numerical order. You may not talk at any time during this task. You have one minute to get yourselves in order.

Team Tally

	1	2	3	4	5	6	7	8	9	10
Creativity										
Communication										
Cooperation										

Total points: _____

Throw in the Towel

Materials

    1 roll of masking tape
    1 yardstick
    3 buckets
    25 tennis balls in a container
    1 bath towel

Set Up

Tape a start line on the floor. Place one bucket 10 feet (3 m) from the start line, another 15 feet (4.6 m) from the line, and a third bucket 20 feet (6 m) from the start line, as shown in the diagram. Set the container of tennis balls near the start line. Assemble the team near the start line and give them the towel. Read the team instructions out loud.

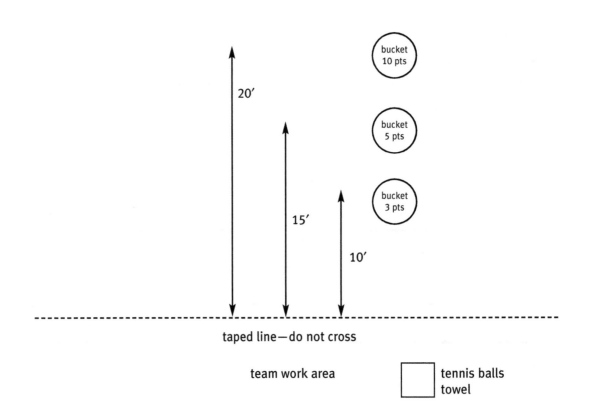

Team Instructions

Your task is to move as many tennis balls as possible across the line taped on the floor and into the buckets, using only the towel to launch the balls. During this task, you may not step over the line at any time. No team member may launch two balls in a row, and launchers may not directly touch the tennis balls. You have three minutes to move as many balls as possible. You will receive three bonus points for every tennis ball in the nearest bucket, five bonus points for balls in the next bucket, and ten bonus points for the bucket farthest away.

Team Tally

	1	2	3	4	5	6	7	8	9	10
Creativity										
Communication										
Cooperation										

Bonus points: _____ balls in first bucket x 3 =

_____ balls in second bucket x 5

_____ balls in third bucket x 10 =

Total points:

Outwit the Sharks

Materials

Index cards, 1 for each team member

1 marker or felt-tipped pen

1 long, horizontal surface about 10 in. (25.4 cm) wide, such as a bleacher seat, a fallen log, or a planter box edge (if none of these is available, run two lines of masking tape, 10 in. [25.4 cm] apart, on the floor)

Set Up

Number the index cards in sequence, beginning with number one. Give one card to each team member. Ask the team members to line up in order on the bleacher seat according to the numbers on their cards. Position yourself at the end of the line, near the highest number. Read the team instructions out loud.

Team Instructions

Your group has tickets to see the shark show at marine land! You've safely crossed the bridge that spans shark bay, but now the crowds are causing a backup over the shark tank. You can't move forward until you turn in your tickets. In order to get moving, you must hand your tickets to me in numerical order, beginning with the number one ticket. As team members give me the proper ticket, they may step off the bridge. But be careful: anyone who falls off the bridge will become shark bait! Team members who fall may not get back on the bridge. You will receive twenty bonus points if all the team members turn in their tickets in the proper order. There is no time limit for solving this task.

Team Tip

Most teams will do the expected and solve this challenge by working cooperatively to pass one another on the narrow bridge. Wonderful! But some teams, using their innate wisdom and quick thinking skills, will do something simpler: switch numbered cards. Obviously, either is a fair solution. If you have kids clever enough to pass the cards to solve the challenge, offer them an additional ten bonus points, then try the task again, adding the caveat that cards cannot be swapped.

Team Tally

	1	2	3	4	5	6	7	8	9	10
Creativity										
Communication										
Cooperation										

Bonus points: 20 bonus points if the entire team turns in tickets in the proper order

Total points:

Use Your Noodle

Materials

Foam swimming pool noodles, cut in half (you'll need one half noodle for each team member)

1 roll of masking tape

20 tennis balls

1 5-gal (19 L) bucket

Set Up

Use the masking tape to mark a line around the center of each half noodle. Scatter the tennis balls on the floor in an area roughly 20 feet (6 m) square. Place the bucket in the center of the space. Give each team member a noodle. Read the team instructions out loud.

Team Instructions

Your task is to move as many tennis balls as possible into the bucket in five minutes. You may not touch the tennis balls with any part of your body. You must use only the noodles to move the tennis balls. You can hold onto only one end of the noodle; your hands must not cross the line taped on the noodle at any time. You will be notified when you have one minute remaining. You will receive two bonus points for every tennis ball in the bucket at the end of time.

Variation

Try it with balloons, ping-pong balls, or even empty water bottles.

Team Tally

	1	2	3	4	5	6	7	8	9	10
Creativity										
Communication										
Cooperation										

Bonus points: Number of tennis balls in the bucket _____ x 2 = _____

Total points: _____

Magic Carpet

Materials

    12-in. square of cardboard, 1 for each team member

    1 roll of masking tape

    1 yardstick

Set Up

Tape two lines on the floor, about 15 feet (4.6 m) apart, to create a mock gorge. Assemble the team on one side of the gorge and give each participant a piece of cardboard. Be prepared to remove unattended magic carpets during the task. Read the team instructions out loud.

Team Instructions

Your team is stranded and must figure out a way to cross the deep gorge ahead of you. You each have a magic carpet that will support weight as you attempt to cross the gorge. You must not leave your magic carpet unattended, or the raven (team leader) that inhabits the gorge will swoop in and take it. You have ten minutes to traverse the gorge. You will be notified when there are three minutes remaining and again when there is one minute remaining. You will receive twenty bonus points if you successfully move the entire team across the gorge.

Team Tally

	1	2	3	4	5	6	7	8	9	10
Creativity										
Communication										
Cooperation										

Bonus points: 20 bonus points if the entire team makes it across the gorge

Total points:

Roll It Along

Materials

Cardboard tubes (paper towel size), 1 for each team member

1 marble

1 paper cup

Set Up

Assemble the materials. Cut each cardboard tube in half lengthwise to create a trough. Line the team up, arm's length apart. Give the marble and one trough to the player at one end of the line. Give the paper cup and one trough to the player at the opposite end of the line. Give all of the other participants two cardboard troughs. Read the team instructions out loud.

Team Instructions

Your task is to move the marble from the start to the end of the line and into the cup. Along the way, the marble must travel through every trough. You may not touch the marble at any time during its travels. If at any time the marble falls to the floor, you may pick it up and start the task over from the beginning. You have four minutes to complete this task. You will be notified when there is one minute remaining. You will receive ten bonus points if you successfully complete this task.

Team Tally

	1	2	3	4	5	6	7	8	9	10
Creativity										
Communication										
Cooperation										

Bonus points: 10 bonus points if the marble makes it to the cup

Total points:

Circle the Group

Materials

1 20-ft (6-m) length of vacuum hose (available at
hardware stores)

1 large marble

Set Up

Assemble the materials. Arrange the team in a circle, facing the center. Wrap the hose around the outside of the circle at waist level, making sure that the ends meet. Instruct participants to hold the hose with both hands. Give the marble to the person nearest the hose ends. Read the team instructions out loud.

Team Instructions

Your task is to move a marble all the way through the hose that is circling your group in less than three minutes. Your hands must remain on the hose at all times, and the hose must remain touching every team member's waist. You must remain in a circle at all times. You will be notified when there are thirty seconds remaining. You will receive ten bonus points if the marble makes it all the way around the circle.

Team Tally

	1	2	3	4	5	6	7	8	9	10
Creativity										
Communication										
Cooperation										

Bonus points: 10 bonus points if the marble circles the group

Total points:

Ping-Pong Ball Overflow

Materials

1 empty 2-gal (7.8-L) bucket
1 5-gal (19-L) bucket, filled with water
1 ping-pong ball
1 yardstick
Plastic or paper cups, 1 for each participant

Set Up

Put the ping-pong ball in the empty bucket. Set the bucket in the center of an open area, outside. Set the bucket full of water 20 feet (6 m) away. Gather the team near the bucket with the ping-pong ball and give each player a paper cup. Read the team instructions out loud.

Team Instructions

Your task is to float the ping-pong ball out of the bucket. You each have a paper cup with which to move water. You may retrieve water only from the bucketful of water standing 20 feet (6 m) away. You may not at any time touch the ping-pong ball or its bucket. You have four minutes to successfully complete the challenge. You will be notified when you have one minute remaining. You will receive ten bonus points if the ping-pong ball is out of the empty bucket at the end of time.

Variation

Add a twist to the task with this limitation: if your cup is full of water, your feet may not move. If a player moves his or her feet with a full cup of water, the player will be eliminated.

Team Tally

	1	2	3	4	5	6	7	8	9	10
Creativity										
Communication										
Cooperation										

Bonus points: 10 bonus points if the ping-pong ball is out of its bucket

Total points:

Put on Your Shoes

Materials

Blindfolds, 1 for each team member

Set Up

Arrange the team members in a large circle (at least 15 feet [4.6 m] across). Ask them to remove their shoes and toss them into the center of the circle. Blindfold all team members. Read the team instructions out loud.

Team Instructions

You have three minutes to find and put on your shoes. Shoes must be completely on and laced or secured appropriately. You may not talk at any time during this task. You will receive ten bonus points if you successfully complete the task in the time allowed.

Team Tally

	1	2	3	4	5	6	7	8	9	10
Creativity										
Communication										
Cooperation										

Bonus points: 10 bonus points if your entire team has on the appropriate shoes

Total points:

It's a Toss Up

Materials

Balls, 1 for each team member; various sizes will work

Set Up

Gather the materials. In a large area outdoors, arrange the team in a circle. Give each participant a ball. Read the team instructions out loud.

Team Instructions

You each have a ball of some sort. Your task is to toss your ball a minimum of 5 feet (1.5 m) into the air and to catch a different ball. To make it easier, you should choose a team leader to tell the team when to toss the balls. You have five minutes to work toward the final goal of each team member catching a different ball, without any balls touching the ground. You will receive twenty bonus points if you succeed.

Team Tally

	1	2	3	4	5	6	7	8	9	10
Creativity										
Communication										
Cooperation										

Bonus points: 20 bonus points if all the balls are caught

Total points:

Loop the Group

Materials

2   6-ft (1.8-m) lengths of cotton rope, tied into loops

Set Up

Provide a large space in which the team can work. Ask the team to form a circle. Place one loop of rope over the arm of one of the players and another over the arm of another player, who is standing roughly opposite the first player in the circle. Now, have the team hold hands. Read the team instructions out loud.

Team Instructions

There are two loops of rope hanging from the arms of your group. The loops must trade places in the circle during this task. You have three minutes to move the loops of rope from their original place in the circle and into the space held by the other loop. You may not release your grasped hands at any time during this task. You will receive ten bonus points if the task is successfully accomplished.

Variation

Instead of having the loops trade places in the circle, ask the team to send both of the loops on a complete circuit of the group, returning to their original starting place without touching each other.

Team Tally

	1	2	3	4	5	6	7	8	9	10
Creativity										
Communication										
Cooperation										

Bonus points: 10 bonus points if both loops trade places in the circle

Total points:

Balloon Shuffle

Materials

20 inflated balloons in a large plastic garbage bag
1 roll of masking tape
1 yardstick

Set Up

Put the inflated balloons in the large garbage bag. Tape a start line on the floor. Tape a finish line on the floor about 10 feet (3 m) away; allow about

5 feet (1.5 m) of empty space across both the start and finish line, as shown in the diagram. Place the balloons at the start line and assemble the team nearby. Read the team instructions out loud.

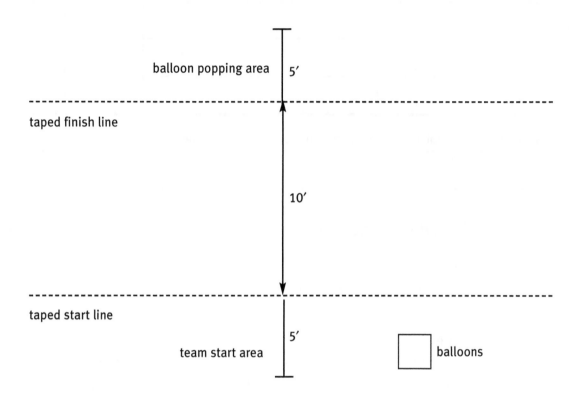

Team Instructions

You have four minutes to move as many balloons as possible from the start line to the finish line. Only two people can be in the area between the start and finish lines at one time. After leaving the start area, players may not touch the balloons with their hands, feet, or mouth. Once a balloon crosses the finish line, it must be popped (remember—no hands, feet, or mouths!)

in order to receive a score. After time expires, you will receive two bonus points for every popped balloon across the finish line.

Team Tally

	1	2	3	4	5	6	7	8	9	10
Creativity										
Communication										
Cooperation										

Bonus points: 2 bonus points per popped balloon across the finish line

Total points:

Limited Movement

Materials

Bouncy balls, 1 for each team member

Set Up

Assemble the materials and provide plenty of space for the team to move around. This activity works best outside or in a gym. Read the team instructions out loud.

Team Instructions

You each have a ball. You may not talk at any time during this task. You are to bounce your ball without stopping until one person on the team chooses to stop. When one person stops bouncing, the entire group should stop bouncing. You must pay close attention to each of your teammates so that the entire group stops bouncing as close to the same time as possible. You have four minutes to cease bouncing as many times as possible. You may not resume bouncing until everyone on the team has stopped. You will receive two bonus points each time you completely cease bouncing.

Team Tally

	1	2	3	4	5	6	7	8	9	10
Creativity										
Communication										
Cooperation										

Bonus points: Number of times bouncing stops _____ x 2

Total points:

A Visit to the Zoo

Materials

1 empty water bottle

1 paper cup

Set Up

Gather the materials and provide ample room in which the team can work. Read the construction materials list and team instructions out loud.

Team Instructions

Choose two team members to portray a day at the zoo. One player must hold the paper cup; the other will hold the plastic bottle. The two players have two minutes to plan a scene from a zoo visit and two minutes to act out the scene for the audience. But wait! There's a catch. The two participants portraying the zoo visit may talk, but they cannot move without help.

Two additional team members must move the actors to match the ongoing dialogue. You will receive twenty bonus points if your scene includes an unexpected event.

Team Tally

	1	2	3	4	5	6	7	8	9	10
Creativity										
Communication										
Cooperation										

Bonus points: 20 bonus points if an unexpected event occurs

Total points:

Strike a Pose

Materials

11 slips of paper

1 marker or felt-tipped pen

1 bowl

Set Up

On strips of paper, write the following: surfing, baseball, typing, riding a bike, talking on the phone, flying, digging, climbing, eating, dancing, and reading. Place the strips of paper in a bowl. Allow ample room in which the team can perform. Read the team instructions out loud.

Team Instructions

Each strip of paper in the bowl has an activity written on it. You must choose two team members at a time to portray the activities written on the strips of paper in the bowl. One of the two players will choose a strip of paper from the bowl and secretly read it. The player will then move his or her partner into poses that express the activity, refraining from gesturing, talking, or showing the partner how to move. The rest of the participants will try to guess the activity portrayed. Each time an activity is correctly guessed, you may change places. You have six minutes to guess as many activities as possible. You will receive five bonus points for every correctly guessed activity.

Team Tally

	1	2	3	4	5	6	7	8	9	10
Creativity										
Communication										
Cooperation										

Bonus points: Number of correct guesses _____ x 5 = _____

Total points: _____

Cross the Chasm

Materials

2 boards, 8 to 10 ft (2.4 to 3 m) long

1 yardstick

5 paper plates

Set Up

To set up this task, you can use 2-by-4-foot (0.6-by-1.2 m) boards from a lumberyard, or if you have access to balance beams, those will work as well. Place the boards on the ground so that they resemble a "V" shape (though they won't actually be touching), with the boards about 3 feet (0.9 m) apart at one end and about 6 feet (1.8 m) apart at the opposite end. Read the team instructions out loud.

Team Instructions

You have made a rare archaeological discovery: ancient dinnerware! You must safely deliver five ancient plates across a chasm, spanned by the two boards in front of you. Only one person at a time can stand on each board. Once a participant steps onto a board, he or she may not step off of the board until reaching the other end. For safety reasons, you must cross the chasm two at a time and must maintain physical contact with your partner at all times. You must move the ancient dinnerware across the chasm without damaging or dropping it. There is no time limit for this task. You will receive ten bonus points if you successfully move all of the plates and the entire team across the chasm.

Team Tally

	1	2	3	4	5	6	7	8	9	10
Creativity										
Communication										
Cooperation										

Bonus points: 10 bonus points for a successful crossing

Total points:

8

Show Me the Funny

Improv Hilarity at Its Best

Using improvisational skills, your team will learn to work together toward some fun and funny solutions to hypothetical situations. The story starters that you'll find near the beginning of this chapter are great warm-ups for kids who haven't had much experience with improv. Story starters are simple prompts that will get your team members thinking creatively and help them to become familiar with the concept of improvising as a group and thinking on their feet. The bulk of this chapter, however, includes tasks that require teammates to use various materials and their improvisational skills to create an original presentation, complete with props.

With these activities, your group will learn to respond immediately and creatively to a mock situation. Whether it is creating an advertisement, petitioning for a new law, or welcoming people to the neighborhood, these activities require fast thinking and a willingness to get a little bit silly. Since each presentation is unscripted, none of the members of your team will know exactly what to expect from the others, meaning that all participants need to be prepared for anything as they plan and perform. The necessary collaboration between teammates will improve their cooperation skills, giving them a better understanding of the importance of working well with others.

As you'd expect, some of the players will at first hesitate to participate with abandon. But it won't take long for them to dismiss their inhibitions and come to the realization that it's okay to be silly. Once they do, the possibilities for creative interpretation and problem solving are endless.

Story Starters

Story starters are a quick, easy way for groups to practice thinking on their feet. Some of the story starters are believable situations that the team might deal with in real life. Others are ludicrous, imaginary situations, which make the role-playing even more challenging.

Encourage your team members to get wild with their interpretations of these events. You want them to start thinking in a creative fashion. The reality is, maybe they actually would end up fighting over movies in a video store, as suggested in one of the story starters that follow; however, you certainly don't want to watch two minutes of mock arguments. The whole point of this activity is to get kids thinking of outlandish solutions and scenes. Rather than fighting, what if they solved the hypothetical problem by ditching their favorite movies and then working together to create a home video comprised of team-performed events from each of those movies? Now, that would be creative!

For each story starter, allow the teammates one minute to plan their scene and two minutes to perform. No scoring is necessary here, but be certain to allow them some time to discuss how well they did after their performance.

Team Instructions

You have one minute to plan and two minutes to perform a skit featuring one of the following situations:

- Your group is at the video store to choose a movie, but each person wants to take a different movie home.
- A group of kids is having a bubble-gum blowing contest, but two of the kids accidentally blow their gum onto the ground.
- One member of your group is at the dentist having a tooth pulled. The dentist forgot to use Novocain.

- Your group is at the library. One member refuses to lower her voice, incurring the wrath of the librarian.
- At a birthday party attended by your group, one child gives a mouse as a gift.
- Every member of your team is reading the same book. The setting is a place called Star Crest, and each of you imagines Star Crest differently. At a book club meeting, you all debate about which of you is correct.
- Walking down the street, a member of your group finds a wallet with five thousand dollars in it.
- At the ice cream parlor, your team has just enough money to buy one sundae that you all will share. Each of you wants a different flavor of ice cream and half of you don't want whipped cream.
- Your group is visiting a farm. When you all sit down to have breakfast, your host explains that if you want milk on your cereal, you'll have to go milk the cow.
- One member of your group is lost in a vacation town. Every person he asks gives him different directions back to his hotel.
- While your team dines at a restaurant, the waiter brings one teammate a bowl of soup with a fly in it. When asked to replace it with another bowl, the waiter refuses.
- Your group receives a mysterious message promising fortune if you all meet someone after dark in an alley. Most of you are curious, one person wants to go, and another is refusing for safety reasons.
- At a store, the clerk is dressed oddly. After further discussion, your team discovers that she believes she is Snow White.
- The phone rings and it is the president of the United States, who asks to be put on speakerphone to talk to your whole group.
- A cat is stuck in a tree, but the fire department is busy fighting a fire.
- Your group is visiting a farm and goes out to collect eggs from the chicken coop. One teammate discovers a golden egg.
- While your team is riding the bus, the driver runs a red light and hits a pedestrian.

- Your group is walking through the jungle when you all hear something rustling in the underbrush nearby.
- Your group is at a local skateboard park when another kid—who is not wearing a helmet—falls down and is badly hurt.
- Your group is attending a concert. One of the members of your group falls asleep and begins snoring loudly.
- One member of your group is having a rough time with her math work, missing all but one of the answers on a test.
- While your team is riding the bus, someone makes an embarrassing noise.
- Your team is attending a tournament and you all have stored your stuff in a locker. When the team goes to get your belongings at the end of the day, you all realize that nobody knows the combination.
- At the beach, your team sets up an umbrella and blanket, then heads off to swim. When you all come back, your stuff is gone.
- Walking down the street to an important meeting, a torrential rain begins. The team has only one umbrella for everyone.
- Your team is at a restaurant ordering breakfast. Your waitress keeps making mistakes as she writes down each person's order. When people try to correct her, she keeps repeating, "It's not your turn. I'll be with you in a moment."
- Your team is stuck in an elevator, and you all discover that the emergency phone doesn't work.
- Your team is having trouble deciding how to spend the afternoon. One person wants to watch a movie, another wants to go to the park, and yet another wants to go swimming.
- Your group is hiking through the woods when you all pass a toad by the side of the path. You all can't believe it when the toad says, "Hey, watch where you're going!"
- On an airplane, your team is seated next to a large man who is snoring very loudly. Nothing any of you do will wake him or make him stop snoring.

- Sitting in a doughnut shop, your team notices that one customer has ordered—and eaten—nine doughnuts, and he is beginning to look a bit sick.
- By chance, everyone in your group is reading the same book. Walking through a tunnel, you find that you've been transported to a scene from the book.
- Your team receives a phone call from the police chief, notifying you that you have all received an award for bravery in the face of danger. None of you can figure out why the team has received this award.
- Your group finds a dog running loose on a playground. When someone checks the dog's tags, you all recognize the name of someone very famous.
- Flipping through a magazine, a team member recognizes a picture of one of his or her classmates.
- Standing outside, while your group is debating the best kind of pizza, a brightly colored parrot lands on the head of one of your teammates.
- You are visiting a museum full of priceless artifacts. One member of your team trips and knocks over a display, breaking a vase. The museum's curator is furious, but remembers what it was like to be a kid.

Improvisational Tasks

When given familiar materials to create props for some of these tasks, teammates will build on their ability to create something from nothing. Other tasks implement an element of surprise, as participants plan a presentation that includes elements unknown until the moment they are to be used. In all cases, teams will plan a story and fabricate a solution to a variety of different dilemmas. These activities will teach kids to think on their feet and to incorporate unplanned elements into each performance.

Tell a Story with a Twist

Materials

Small slips of paper
1 marker or felt-tipped pen
1 bowl

Set Up

On small strips of paper, write the names of about a dozen popular movies that your group is likely to have seen. Place the strips of paper into the bowl. Read the team instructions out loud.

Team Instructions

Choose one individual to portray a character from a movie. The chosen individual will choose a strip of paper from the bowl. On it is the title of a movie. The individual will portray a character from the movie written on the strip of paper. The remaining members of the group will select a second strip of paper. They will choose characters and a scene from the movie written on their strip of paper. The individual and the group will work together and discuss the possibilities for solving this task. You have four minutes to plan a presentation explaining how the individual character ended up in the wrong movie. You will be notified when you have only one minute of planning time remaining. At the end of the planning time, you will have an additional two minutes to present your scene. You will receive ten bonus points if every member of your team has a recognizable part in the production.

Team Tally

	1	2	3	4	5	6	7	8	9	10
Creativity										
Communication										
Cooperation										

Bonus points: 10 points if every player has a recognizable part

Total points:

Portray a Night at the Movies

Materials

    1 paper lunch sack

    3 drinking straws

    1 sheet of paper

    1 pair of glasses

Set Up

Place all of the materials into the lunch sack and provide a space for the presentation. Read the list of materials and the team instructions out loud.

Team Instructions

Your task is to portray a night at the movies. You may use the lunch bag and all of the materials it holds in your presentation. You have four minutes to plan your presentation and one minute to present your solution to the judge. You may portray animate or inanimate objects. Remember, there's more to the movie theater than the audience, and creativity counts. You will be notified when you have one minute of planning time remaining. You will then have two minutes to present your show.

Team Tally

	1	2	3	4	5	6	7	8	9	10
Creativity										
Communication										
Cooperation										

Total points: _____

> ### Team Tip
>
> *Give participants the opportunity to try it again if they have trouble jumping right into their presentation. Ask them to try a different perspective. If they need examples, remind them that a night at the movies means something different for everyone, depending upon the perspective. The mouse that lives in the wall will see it quite differently than the usher at the door.*

Create an Animal

Materials

Sheets of newspaper, 1 for each team member
Sheets of mailing labels, 1 for each team member

Set Up

Place the mailing labels on a table and give each team member a sheet of newspaper. Read the team instructions out loud.

Team Instructions

Each of you has one sheet of newspaper and one sheet of mailing labels. In the first part of this task, each team member—working individually—will have two minutes to construct an animal part. At the end of the first two minutes, your team will have two more minutes to work together to combine all of the body parts into one new animal. You may not talk at any time during the building phase of this task. You will be notified when only thirty seconds of building time remain. At the end of the building time, your team will have one minute to present the animal to the zookeeper (team leader). The zookeeper will be interested in hearing about the animal's habits, natural habitat, and physical characteristics. If, at the end of your presentation, you have convinced the zookeeper to buy your animal, you will receive twenty bonus points.

Team Tally

	1	2	3	4	5	6	7	8	9	10
Creativity										
Communication										
Cooperation										

Bonus points: 20 bonus points if the zookeeper makes a purchase

Total points:

Tell a Story from a Magazine

Materials

Old magazines, 1 for each team member

Set Up

Give one old magazine to each player. Provide ample room in which the team can work. Read the team instructions out loud.

Team Instructions

You each have a magazine. You have five minutes to tear pictures or phrases out of the magazines and plan a skit. You will be notified when you have one minute remaining. When time is up, you have two minutes to use every picture or phrase in a coherent performance. You will lose three points for every torn-out picture or phrase that is *not* incorporated into the story.

Team Tally

	1	2	3	4	5	6	7	8	9	10
Creativity										
Communication										
Cooperation										

Negative points: Number of pictures or phrases not used in story _____ x 3 =

Total points:

Make a Musical Instrument

Materials

Full sheets of newspaper, 1 for each team member

1 sheet of sticky dots

Set Up

Gather the materials. Set the sticky dots on a table and give each team member a sheet of newspaper. Read the team instructions out loud.

Team Instructions

You each have a sheet of newspaper. There are sticky dots on the table that are for everyone to use. You have three minutes to create a musical instrument out of your sheet of paper. You may not talk at any time as you work. When building time expires, you will have one minute to perform a song using your instruments. You will be notified when you have thirty seconds of building time remaining. You will receive five bonus points for each original instrument; duplicate instruments will not receive points.

Team Tally

	1	2	3	4	5	6	7	8	9	10
Creativity										
Communication										
Cooperation										

Bonus points: Number of original instruments _____ x 5 =

Total points:

Explain the Shades

Materials

1 6-in.- (15-cm-) high stack of newspapers

1 roll of masking tape

Pairs of sunglasses, 1 for each team member

Set Up

Place all of the materials on a table. Read the list of materials and the team instructions out loud.

Team Instructions

It is midnight and completely dark. Using the materials provided, plan a presentation explaining why you are all wearing your sunglasses at night. You have five minutes to plan your presentation and create costumes and props. You will be notified when you have one minute of planning time remaining. When building time expires, you will tell your story. You will receive ten bonus points for every minute of your presentation.

Team Tally

	1	2	3	4	5	6	7	8	9	10
Creativity										
Communication										
Cooperation										

Bonus points: Length of presentation in minutes _____ x 10 = _____

Total points: _____

Invent a Letter

Materials

    5 mailing labels
    2 sheets of copy paper
    3 sheets of newspaper
    1 marker*
*May not be altered

Set Up

Place all of the materials on a table. Read the list of materials and the team instructions out loud.

Team Instructions

The president has decided to add a twenty-seventh letter to the alphabet. Your assignment is to invent the letter that will be the most beneficial. You have three minutes to decide upon the sound and symbol for your new letter. Then, it's time to present your letter to the president. You will have one minute to convince him that your letter is the best. You will receive ten bonus points if your letter is deemed to be a useful addition to the English language.

Team Tally

	1	2	3	4	5	6	7	8	9	10
Creativity										
Communication										
Cooperation										

Bonus points: 10 bonus points if the letter is useful

Total points:

Animal Antics

Materials

Slips of paper, 1 for each team member
Pens, 1 for each team member
10 toothpicks
2 pebbles

Set Up

Place the materials on a table and provide ample room for some animal action. Ask the team members to secretly write their favorite animal on a slip of paper. Read the list of materials and the team instructions out loud.

Team Instructions

As a team, you must guess each of your teammates' favorite animals. You have three minutes to pass the information in silence, using the pebbles and toothpicks. You will be notified when you have thirty seconds remaining.

When time is up, two team members will announce the favorite animals of every other member of the team. The announcers may not divulge their own favorite animal. For each correct guess, your team will earn five bonus points.

Team Tally

	1	2	3	4	5	6	7	8	9	10
Creativity										
Communication										
Cooperation										

Bonus points: Number of animals guessed correctly _____ x 5 = _____

Total points: _____

Create a Character

Materials

2 rolls of masking tape
The Sunday paper

Set Up

Place the materials on a table and allow ample room in which the team can work. Read the list of materials and the team instructions out loud.

Team Instructions

You have five minutes to create a hat for each team member. During this time, you will construct hats and discuss the individual personas that each team member will portray. At the end of the five-minute period, you will have two minutes to introduce each character to the judge. You will receive five bonus points for each visibly different hat.

Team Tally

	1	2	3	4	5	6	7	8	9	10
Creativity										
Communication										
Cooperation										

Bonus points: Number of visibly different hats _____ x 5 = _____

Total points: _____

What's Going On?

Materials

1 box

1 piece of paper

4 pieces of recycled cardboard

10 mailing labels

2 magazines

Scissors*

*May not be altered

Set Up

Place all of the materials in a box on a table. Divide the team into two groups: Group A and Group B. Provide a separate space in which each group can work. Read the list of materials and the team instructions out loud.

Team Instructions

This task has two parts. In part one, Group A has five minutes to create a pretend device that might be used to enhance vision, using the materials provided. During this time, Group B will plan a performance. In part two,

Group B has two minutes to act out and silently tell their story. Group A will watch Group B through their vision enhancer. While watching, Group A will give a play-by-play description of Group B's performance.

Team Tally

	1	2	3	4	5	6	7	8	9	10
Creativity										
Communication										
Cooperation										

Total points:

Create an Advertisement

Materials

2 cups (460 mL) dry beans

1 cardboard tube

1 10-x-15-in. (25.4-x-38-cm) piece of cardboard

5 straws

1 sheet of paper

1 12-in. (30-cm) piece of string

1 egg carton

1 pen*

Scissors*

*May not be altered

Set Up

Place all the materials on a large table. Read the list of materials and the team instructions out loud.

Team Instructions

Your task is to sell a product. You have three minutes to create a two- or three-dimensional advertisement for a product of your choice. Upon completion of your advertisement, you will have one minute to present your product to the judge. Remember, creativity counts! You will receive ten bonus points if the judge thinks he or she might buy the product someday.

Team Tally

	1	2	3	4	5	6	7	8	9	10
Creativity										
Communication										
Cooperation										

Bonus points: 10 bonus points for a successful sales pitch

Total points:

Make the Life of a Teacher Easier

Materials

3 paper napkins

2 12-in. (30-cm) lengths of string

5 corks

15 toothpicks

5 paper cups

10 spaghetti noodles

1 egg carton

Set Up

Place all the materials on a large table. Read the list of materials and the team instructions out loud.

Team Instructions

You have two minutes to plan without touching the materials. You then have five minutes to build a new tool or machine that will make a teacher's job easier to do. At the end of the allotted building time, your team will give a one-minute presentation to introduce the invention and explain how it works and how it will help a teacher. You will receive ten bonus points if the invention addresses and solves a problem unique to teachers.

Team Tally

	1	2	3	4	5	6	7	8	9	10
Creativity										
Communication										
Cooperation										

Bonus points: 10 bonus points for a useful invention

Total points:

Create an Object from Aluminum Foil

Materials

12-in. (30-cm) squares of aluminum foil, 1 for each team member

Set Up

Sit the team members in a circle, with their backs to the center of the circle, and hand each person a sheet of aluminum foil. Read the team instructions out loud.

Team Instructions

You each have a sheet of aluminum foil. You have two minutes to create something with your foil. You will be notified when you have only thirty seconds of building time remaining. You may not talk during the building time. When time expires, turn and face the center of the circle. Now, you will each pass your creation to the person on your right and take turns telling about the new item you are holding.

Team Tally

	1	2	3	4	5	6	7	8	9	10
Creativity										
Communication										
Cooperation										

Total points: _____

Market Mondo Milk

Materials

1 empty milk carton

3 sheets of paper

5 marshmallows

5 drinking straws

1 newspaper page

1 sheet of sticky dots

1 paper party hat

Markers*

*May not be altered

Set Up

Place all of the materials on a table. Read the list of materials and the team instructions out loud.

Team Instructions

After much experimentation, a chemist has developed a dairy-free drink called Mondo Milk. Made strictly in a laboratory setting, the milk will replace the need for dairy cows. Better yet, the chemist claims that the manufactured milk will improve muscle mass, lower cholesterol, and increase the amount of chocolate the average person can safely consume. Critics of Mondo Milk are concerned about the demise of the dairy cow. Your team will unveil the new drink at a food convention. You have five minutes to plan a presentation selling the attendees on the benefits of this new product. Your presentation must include a slogan for Mondo Milk and a jingle. When time expires, you will have two minutes to perform your presentation. You will receive ten bonus points if every team member participates in the presentation.

Team Tally

	1	2	3	4	5	6	7	8	9	10
Creativity										
Communication										
Cooperation										

Bonus points: 10 bonus points for full participation

Total points:

Equip a College Dorm Room

Materials

    1 egg carton
    15 drinking straws

1 sheet of mailing labels

5 paper cups

2 paper plates

3 erasers

25 toothpicks

10 index cards

Set Up

Place all of the materials on a table. Read the list of materials and the team instructions out loud.

Team Instructions

College dorm rooms are famous for being tiny, yet residents often want to bring all the comforts of home with them. Microwaves have made their way to dorm rooms, making it easy to warm up food, but they can't replicate Mom's home cooking. In this task, you must determine what one food item would make a college freshman's dorm stay more palatable and then create a device that will produce that food item. But your job doesn't end there. You must convince the incoming freshmen that your device will offer all of the comforts of home. Remember, the device needs to fit in a small space! You have five minutes to create your device and plan a skit and three minutes to perform. You will receive ten bonus points if you convince the judge that your device is worth buying.

Team Tally

	1	2	3	4	5	6	7	8	9	10
Creativity										
Communication										
Cooperation										

Bonus points: 10 bonus points for a convincing performance

Total points:

Create a Superhero

Materials

1 plastic grocery bag

5 mailing labels

1 12-in. (30-cm) piece of string

2 clothespins

10 paper clips

10 straws

1 balloon

1 sheet of newspaper

Set Up

Place all of the materials into the plastic grocery bag. Provide an area in which the team can work. Read the list of materials and the team instructions out loud.

Team Instructions

Your task is to create a superhero using the materials given. You have five minutes to discuss the problem and create your superhero. You will be notified when only one minute of planning time remains. You will then have two minutes to tell a story about your superhero, explain his or her super powers, and tell how the super powers can save the world. You will receive ten bonus points if your story makes the judge laugh aloud.

Team Tally

	1	2	3	4	5	6	7	8	9	10
Creativity										
Communication										
Cooperation										

Bonus points: 10 bonus points for laughter

Total points:

Save Yourselves from Becoming Shark Bait!

Materials

   1 brown paper bag

   1 envelope

   1 3-in. (7.6-cm) piece of string

   5 paper cups

   1 tennis ball*

   1 scarf*

   1 hat*

*May not be altered

Set Up

Place all of the materials in the brown paper bag. Provide an open area in which the team members can present their solution. Read the list of materials and the team instructions out loud.

Team Instructions

You are stranded on an island surrounded by sharks! You must devise a plan and tell a story about escaping the island without becoming shark bait. In the bag are materials that you can use to tell your story. You may not alter the tennis ball, scarf, or hat. You have five minutes to devise your plan and practice your presentation and two minutes to present your solution to the judge. You will be notified when you have only one minute of planning time remaining. Five bonus points will be given for each full minute of the presentation, up to ten points.

Team Tally

	1	2	3	4	5	6	7	8	9	10
Creativity										
Communication										
Cooperation										

Bonus points: 5 bonus points for each full minute of the presentation (10 points maximum)

Total points:

Sell the Moon

Materials

1 picture of the moon
1 sheet of poster board
Markers*

*May not be altered

Set Up

Place the materials on a table. Read the list of materials and the team instructions out loud.

Team Instructions

Modern technology has finally made travel to the moon possible! Your team has agreed to act as the official travel agent for the lunar trips that are now available to everyone, yet still a bit expensive. Use the materials provided and the next five minutes to create an advertisement that will convince people to spend their hard-earned money on a trip to the moon. You will be notified when you have one minute remaining. When time expires, you have two minutes to present your advertisement.

Team Tally

	1	2	3	4	5	6	7	8	9	10
Creativity										
Communication										
Cooperation										

Total points:

Revolutionize the Year 2100

Materials

1 brown paper bag
1 lump of clay
25 drinking straws

3 small boxes

5 paper cups

10 mailing labels

10 rubber bands

Scissors*

*May not be altered

Set Up

Place all of the materials in a brown paper bag and place the bag on the table. Read the team instructions out loud. Do *not* read the materials list aloud.

Team Instructions

The wheel revolutionized the prehistoric age. The automobile revolutionized the 20th century. Your task is to invent a tool that will revolutionize the world in the year 2100. You have two minutes to discuss the problem. You may not look in the bag of supplies during the two-minute discussion time. After the first two minutes, you have five minutes to build and one minute to present your invention to the judge, using the materials in the paper bag. You will be notified when you have one minute of building time remaining. Your presentation should answer the following questions: Why is this invention important to humans in the year 2100? What will it accomplish? How will it improve life in the future? You will receive ten bonus points if every member of your team is involved in the presentation.

Team Tally

	1	2	3	4	5	6	7	8	9	10
Creativity										
Communication										
Cooperation										

Bonus points: 10 points for full participation

Total points:

Perform a Skit

Materials

Household items, 1 for each team member

Brown paper bags, 1 for each team member

1 roll of masking tape

1 marker or felt-tipped pen

Set Up

Gather the materials. Number each paper bag in order, starting with number one. Place one household item in each bag and tape the bag closed. Give each team member a bag. Read the team instructions out loud.

Team Instructions

You each have a bag. You may not look in the bag. You have four minutes of discussion time in which to develop a skit with a complete story line, including a beginning, middle, and end. You will be notified when you have one minute of planning time remaining. You will then have four minutes to perform your skit. As your story develops, you must open the bags in numerical order and use the item inside in your presentation. You may not open the bag until the moment the items are to be used. Incorporate the items into your skit using their traditional purposes or made-up ones. You will receive twenty bonus points if you manage to use all of the items in your production.

Team Tally

	1	2	3	4	5	6	7	8	9	10
Creativity										
Communication										
Cooperation										

Bonus points: 20 bonus points if all items appeared in the skit

Total points:

Sell Spinach

Materials

1 brown paper bag

1 12-in. (30-cm) square of aluminum foil

2 sheets of copy paper

1 12-in. (30-cm) length of string

3 film canisters

Set Up

Place the materials on a large table. Read the list of materials and the team instructions out loud.

Team Instructions

You have three minutes to create an advertisement for chopped spinach. You will be notified when you have one minute of planning time remaining. At the end of the allotted time, you will have one minute to present your advertisement to the judge. Remember, creativity counts! You will receive ten bonus points if the judge thinks he or she might try your chopped spinach.

Team Tally

	1	2	3	4	5	6	7	8	9	10
Creativity										
Communication										
Cooperation										

Bonus points: 10 bonus points if the judge might try it

Total points:

Uncover History at an Archaeological Dig

Materials

1 large box

1 egg carton

1 paper clip

1 small toy figure

1 miniature toy car

1 battery

1 eraser

1 plastic milk jug

1 computer disk

Set Up

Put all of the materials into the large box. Assemble the team near the box. Read the team instructions out loud.

Team Instructions

The year is 3010. Your team of archaeologists has just discovered the remains of an ancient civilization, dating back to the year 2000. After a number of days in the hot, dry dust, you have unearthed some interesting items that will give future generations a glimpse into life in the year 2000. You have three minutes to explore the artifacts in the box and prepare for the press conference announcing this great discovery. You will be notified when you have one minute of planning time remaining. Following the preview, you have three more minutes to present your findings—along with detailed descriptions of each artifact and what it was used for—to the press. Remember, the items you have discovered are a mystery to you. You will receive five bonus points for each plausible description.

Team Tally

	1	2	3	4	5	6	7	8	9	10
Creativity										
Communication										
Cooperation										

Bonus points: 5 bonus points for each believable description

Total points:

There Ought to Be a Law

Materials

1 household item (the more outlandish, the better—for
example, a French fry cutter or a squeegee)

1 sheet of paper

1 book

1 hat

1 empty water bottle

3 sticky dots

1 envelope

Pieces of candy, enough for each team member

Set Up

Place all of the materials on a table and assemble the team nearby. Read the
list of materials and the team instructions out loud.

Team Instructions

From speed limits to curfews, our country has an abundance of laws that
citizens must obey. Laws protect our safety and property and they govern
our country. What law do you think is missing from our world? Your task
is to determine a need for a law and present a clear-cut case for why the

country should implement your law. You have three minutes to develop your new law and two minutes to convince the government (team leader) to add your law to the books. You will be notified when you have one minute of planning time remaining. You will earn twenty bonus points if you use all of the props in your presentation.

Team Tally

	1	2	3	4	5	6	7	8	9	10
Creativity										
Communication										
Cooperation										

Bonus points: 20 bonus points if all the props are used

Total points:

Shipwrecked!

Materials

    1 box

    1 brown paper bag

    1 24-in. (61-cm) length of string

    1 hat

    1 empty water bottle

    1 newspaper page

    3 clothespins

    1 film canister

Set Up

Place the materials in the box and provide ample room in which the team can work. Read the list of materials and the team instructions out loud.

Team Instructions

Your boat has shipwrecked! After floating aimlessly on the ocean for days, you land on an island. Your supplies have dwindled, but you have salvaged some things from the ship. Sitting on the beach, discussing what to do next, you are surprised by a group of natives holding menacing spears. You have four minutes to plan a skit showing how your team will get out of this predicament. You will be notified when you have one minute of planning time remaining. You will then have two minutes to present the skit, showcasing your creative escape to the judge. You will receive ten bonus points if you use all of the props in your presentation.

Team Tally

	1	2	3	4	5	6	7	8	9	10
Creativity										
Communication										
Cooperation										

Bonus points: 10 bonus points if all the props are used

Total points:

Finally, a Cure for the Common Cold!

Materials

1 brown paper bag

1 cardboard tube

1 plastic spoon

1 empty tissue box

5 cotton balls

5 drinking straws

1 orange

Set Up

Place all of the materials in the brown paper bag. Read the list of materials and the team instructions out loud.

Team Instructions

A giant pharmaceutical company has finally found a cure for the common cold. The company chose your team to create an ad campaign encouraging consumers to buy this new medication. You have four minutes to use the materials to create a TV commercial touting the benefits of the medication. Your advertisement should include the name of the new product, the benefits it can provide to sick people, and, of course, the various and many side effects that may be encountered by those who use it. You will be notified when you have one minute of planning time remaining. When time expires, you will have one minute to present your advertisement to the pharmaceutical company for its approval. You will receive ten bonus points if every team member is involved in the presentation.

Team Tally

	1	2	3	4	5	6	7	8	9	10
Creativity										
Communication										
Cooperation										

Bonus points: 10 bonus points for full participation

Total points:

Add-Ons

Materials

12-in. (30-cm) squares of aluminum foil, 1 for each
team member

Set Up

Give each team member a piece of aluminum foil. Arrange the team in a circle on the floor. Read the team instructions out loud.

Team Instructions

You each have a piece of aluminum foil. Working individually, you have one minute to create something—anything—from the foil. At the end of the one-minute building time, one team member will share with the group what his or her creation is. The team member will then pass the creation to the left, where the next person will add his or her creation to it and tell about the resulting creation. You will work your way all the way around the circle in this manner until all of the individual creations are one.

Team Tally

	1	2	3	4	5	6	7	8	9	10
Creativity										
Communication										
Cooperation										

Total points: _____

Celebrate!

Materials

Several sheets of paper

Pens or pencils

Set Up

Place the materials on a table. Read the team instructions out loud.

Team Instructions

Your team has won the World Championship Fluggle-Whumping Contest. It is traditional for the winning team to perform an original celebratory song at the awards ceremony. You have six minutes to write and practice your song. You will be notified when you have one minute of planning time remaining. When time expires, you have two minutes in which to perform your song. You will receive twenty bonus points if your performance includes dancing or choreography.

Team Tally

	1	2	3	4	5	6	7	8	9	10
Creativity										
Communication										
Cooperation										

Bonus points: 20 bonus points for dancing or choreography

Total points:

Happy Birthday!

Materials

1 brown paper bag

5 sheets of paper

1 egg carton

10 drinking straws

2 paper cups

1 box of plastic bandages

1 empty water bottle

1 12-in. (30-cm) square of aluminum foil

1 hat

Set Up

Place all of the materials in the brown paper bag and provide ample room in which the team can work. Read the team instructions out loud.

Team Instructions

You have been invited to a birthday party for a famous person. There's only one problem: you forgot to buy a gift and the party is ready to start. You have five minutes and some miscellaneous items in a bag that you can use to create a gift. As a team, determine who the famous person is and create an appropriate birthday gift for him or her. You will be notified when you have one minute of planning time remaining. When time expires, you have three minutes to portray a scene in which the famous person receives your unique gift. You will receive ten bonus points if the judge laughs aloud.

Team Tally

	1	2	3	4	5	6	7	8	9	10
Creativity										
Communication										
Cooperation										

Bonus points: 10 bonus points for laughter

Total points:

Game Time

Materials

    1 brown paper bag

    3 ping-pong balls

    5 paper cups

    1 3-ft (0.9-m) length of string

    30 drinking straws

    1 cardboard tube

    3 sheets of newspaper

    20 paper clips

Set Up

Place all of the materials in a brown paper bag. Provide the team with a large table on which to work. Read the list of materials and the team instructions out loud.

Team Instructions

Your task is to create a rainy-day tabletop game that will entertain young children. The game must have at least three ways to achieve a score and must take less than ten minutes to play, start to finish. You have seven minutes to plan your game and create a model of it. You will be notified when you have one minute of planning time remaining. At the end of the design time, you have two minutes to exhibit your game and explain the rules. You will receive ten bonus points if the judge understands the rules of the game.

Team Tally

	1	2	3	4	5	6	7	8	9	10
Creativity										
Communication										
Cooperation										

Bonus points: 10 bonus points for clear instructions

Total points:

Zoo Snafu

Materials

    1 pair of sunglasses

    1 stuffed animal

    3 sheets of paper

    1 brown paper bag

    1 envelope

    3 tennis balls

Set Up

Gather the materials and provide ample room in which the team can plan and perform. Read the list of materials and the team instructions out loud.

Team Instructions

There's been a breakout at the zoo and animals are running wild! Just imagine the chaos. The local TV network has just arrived to cover the late breaking news. You must portray the scene for the TV audience that is watching. One person must act as a news correspondent and one will represent an escaped zoo animal. All other participants will act in supporting roles chosen by the team. You have four minutes to plan your presentation and three minutes to present your newscast. You will receive ten bonus points for each full minute of your presentation.

Team Tally

	1	2	3	4	5	6	7	8	9	10
Creativity										
Communication										
Cooperation										

Bonus points: Minutes of the presentation _____ x 10 = _____

Total points: _____

Puppet Play

Materials

2 paper plates

20 paper clips

5 drinking straws

1 sheet of sticky dots

30 toothpicks

5 rubber bands

1 paper towel tube

1 paper cup

Markers*

Scissors*

*May not be altered

Set Up

Place all of the materials on a table. Read the list of materials and the team instructions out loud.

Team Instructions

A large group of preschoolers is expecting to see a puppet show, but the puppet master—along with all of his puppets—has been delayed. Your team must step in to help! You need to think quickly to create puppets from the materials provided. Your show must have a minimum of three puppets and must be nonviolent—these are preschoolers, after all. You have five minutes to create your cast of puppets and plan a presentation that will keep the preschoolers entertained for two minutes. You will receive ten bonus points if your story lasts for the full two minutes.

Team Tally

	1	2	3	4	5	6	7	8	9	10
Creativity										
Communication										
Cooperation										

Bonus points: 10 bonus points if the show goes on for two minutes

Total points:

Welcome Wagon

Materials

  3 paper cups
  1 sheet of mailing labels
  1 paper lunch sack
  2 paper plates
  10 drinking straws
  3 sheets of newspaper
  5 rubber bands

Set Up

Place all of the materials on a table and provide a space for your team to perform. Read the list of materials and the team instructions out loud.

Team Instructions

A new family has moved into the neighborhood! Many communities have a "welcome wagon" group for the purposes of making new residents feel at home. Your task is to create a gift to welcome the family and give them an idea of the fun activities that your town offers. You have five minutes to create an assortment of items to give to the family and one minute to present your gift, along with welcoming wishes. You will receive five bonus points for each useful item included in your welcome gift.

Team Tally

	1	2	3	4	5	6	7	8	9	10
Creativity										
Communication										
Cooperation										

Bonus points: 5 bonus points for each useful gift

Total points:

Create an Olympic Event

Materials

 1 cardboard box

 1 tennis ball

 1 cardboard tube

 3 brown paper bags

 1 small bucket

 1 10-ft. (3-m) length of string

 3 recycled plastic lids

 5 rubber bands

Set Up

Place all of the materials in the cardboard box. Provide the team members with plenty of space in which to work and present their solution. Read the list of materials and the team instructions out loud.

Team Instructions

The International Olympic Committee plans to add a new sport to the Winter Olympics. The committee needs your creative help. Your task is to create and present an entirely new game for the committee to review. The new sporting event must have at least one goal and must include elements from each of the following sports: baseball, football, synchronized swimming, and badminton. You have six minutes to develop the new event and two minutes to present your game—along with a demonstration of the sport—to the International Olympic Committee (team leader). If your game meets all of the required elements, the game will be unveiled during the next Winter Olympics and you'll receive twenty bonus points.

Team Tally

	1	2	3	4	5	6	7	8	9	10
Creativity										
Communication										
Cooperation										

Bonus points: 20 bonus points for a great game

Total points:

Instant Replay

Materials

    3 cardboard tubes

    3 sheets of newspaper

    1 foam pool noodle

    1 brown paper bag

Set Up

Assemble the materials and provide ample room in which the team can perform. Read the list of materials and the team instructions out loud.

Team Instructions

Your task is to re-create and report on a sporting event. One member of your team will act as the sports commentator for the local news station. The sports commentator will report on an unexpected event that occurred during a local game. The rest of the team will act out the event, creating film footage as the commentator shares the details with television viewers. You have five minutes to create your performance. But wait: there's a catch. The film footage of the event must be presented in slow motion. You have two minutes to present your solution.

Team Tally

	1	2	3	4	5	6	7	8	9	10
Creativity										
Communication										
Cooperation										

Total points:

Sell a Shoe

Materials

1 brown paper bag

5 drinking straws

3 sheets of newspaper

1 sheet of sticky dots

1 old shoe

3 cardboard tubes

3 small cardboard boxes

1 empty water bottle

Set Up

Place all of the materials in the brown paper bag and allow ample room in which the team can present its solution. Read the list of materials and the team instructions out loud.

Team Instructions

The Old Woman who lives in a shoe is moving. After years of housing the Old Woman and all of her children, the shoe is pretty worn out. She has asked your team to help sell the shoe. You have five minutes to determine what other nursery rhyme character might buy the shoe and to create a sales pitch aimed directly at him or her, using the materials provided. You will be notified when only one minute of planning time remains. When planning time expires, you will have two minutes to try to sell the shoe. You will receive ten bonus points if all members of your team participate in the presentation.

Team Tally

	1	2	3	4	5	6	7	8	9	10
Creativity										
Communication										
Cooperation										

Bonus points: 10 bonus points for full participation

Total points:

Create Communication

Materials

  1 brown paper bag
  1 cardboard box
  5 recycled plastic lids
  1 5-ft (1.5-m) length of string
  3 paper cups
  1 sheet of newspaper
  10 paper clips
  1 sheet of mailing labels

Set Up

Place the materials in the brown paper bag and assemble the team. Read the list of materials and the team instructions out loud.

Team Instructions

Communication methods have changed much just in the last fifty years. We now have e-mail, cellular phones, and text messaging. Just imagine how things will change in the future! Your task is to look into the future and create an all-new method of communication. You have five minutes to discuss a plan and create a device that people will use to communicate in the year 2055. You will be notified when only one minute of planning time remains. Following the planning time, you will have two minutes to demonstrate your communication method to the judge. You will receive ten bonus points if you use all of the materials in your presentation.

Team Tally

	1	2	3	4	5	6	7	8	9	10
Creativity										
Communication										
Cooperation										

Bonus points: 10 bonus points if all materials are used

Total points:

Go on Safari

Materials

1 plastic grocery bag

5 mailing labels

1 12-in. (30-cm) piece of string

5 index cards

10 paper clips

10 straws

1 balloon

3 cardboard tubes

3 sheets of newspaper

Set Up

Place all of the materials in the plastic bag. Divide the team into two groups: Group A and Group B. Provide a separate space in which each group can work. Read the list of construction materials and the team instructions out loud.

Team Instructions

This task has two parts. In part one, Group A has five minutes to create a camera crew—complete with equipment—that is heading out on safari in search of the elusive three-toed, stripeless zebra. During this time, Group B will prepare a safari scene, including at least one three-toed, stripeless zebra. You will be notified when you have only one minute of planning time remaining. In part two, Group B has two minutes to present its safari scene. The camera crew must capture the scene on film, along with commentary explaining the scene to television viewers around the world. You will receive ten bonus points if the commentary explains why the three-toed, stripeless zebra is so elusive.

Team Tally

	1	2	3	4	5	6	7	8	9	10
Creativity										
Communication										
Cooperation										

Bonus points: 10 bonus points if commentary answers the mystery of the three-toed, stripeless zebra

Total points:

Order Up!

Materials

3 sheets of paper

10 toothpicks

5 bandage strips

1 12-in. (30-cm) square of aluminum foil

2 binder clips

2 cardboard tubes

5 rubber bands

Set Up

Place the materials on a table and allow room in which the team can perform. Read the list of materials and the team instructions out loud. Note to team leader: You'll need a bell or similar noisemaker for your part in this task.

Team Instructions

It's Friday night at the diner and everyone is having a good time—until the milk shake machine breaks down. You have five minutes to create props and plan a scene from the diner that includes at least one police officer. You will be notified when you have one minute of time remaining. Following the planning time, you will have two minutes in which to portray your evening at the diner. But wait: there's a catch. As you perform, you must alternate between sound and silence. A special sound will signal you to move from speaking to silence; you should make the transition as seamless as possible. You will receive ten bonus points if you make it through the silent portions of your performance without uttering a sound.

Team Tally

	1	2	3	4	5	6	7	8	9	10
Creativity										
Communication										
Cooperation										

Bonus points: 10 bonus points for complete silence

Total points:

Create Your Favorite Character from a Book

Materials

1 brown paper bag

3 rolls of toilet paper

1 roll of masking tape

8 drinking straws

1 box of paper clips

Set Up

Place all of the materials in the brown paper bag. Provide ample space for the team's presentation. Read the team instructions out loud.

Team Instructions

You have one minute to plan and four minutes to recreate a character from a book. Your materials are in the paper bag. You may not look in the bag during the one minute planning time. Following the one minute planning time, you will open the bag and use the materials to recreate your character. When time expires, your team will present a scene from the book that includes the chosen character and at least one other character. You will receive ten bonus points for each full minute of your presentation, up to twenty points.

Team Tally

	1	2	3	4	5	6	7	8	9	10
Creativity										
Communication										
Cooperation										

Bonus points: Full minutes of the presentation _____ x 10 = _____

Total points: _____

Talk Show

Materials

Chairs, 1 for each team member

Hats, 1 for each team member

1 book

Candy, 1 piece for each team member

Set Up

Place chairs in an arrangement suitable for an interview—one for each team member. Gather the materials and place them nearby. Read the team instructions out loud.

Team Instructions

Talk shows allow a television host to interview guests, both famous and not so famous. In this task, you will present a morning talk show, complete with a chatty host and several interesting characters. Your show must include a Hollywood hat designer, a local candy maker who thinks his candy is fabulous, and a book author. You have two minutes to study your props and plan a presentation. You will be notified when you have only thirty seconds of planning time remaining. Following planning time, you will have four minutes to create a segment for your talk show. You will receive ten bonus points if every member of your team participates in the show.

Team Tally

	1	2	3	4	5	6	7	8	9	10
Creativity										
Communication										
Cooperation										

Bonus points: 10 bonus points for full participation

Total points:

Airport

Materials

1 paper cup

1 12-in. (30-cm) piece of aluminum foil

20 Styrofoam peanuts

5 drinking straws

10 toothpicks

1 magazine

Set Up

Gather the materials and place them on a table. Provide the team with plenty of space in which to work. Read the list of materials and the team instructions out loud.

Team Instructions

You are traveling to visit your grandma across the country. You are bringing her a kitten as a gift. You have the kitten in a carrier, but the airport personnel won't allow the kitten on the plane until you have a plan for a kitty potty. One of the major concerns is odor. You have two minutes to create a portable litter box and one minute to convince the airline officials to let you board the plane. You will receive ten bonus points if your solution is convincing.

Team Tally

	1	2	3	4	5	6	7	8	9	10
Creativity										
Communication										
Cooperation										

Bonus points: 10 bonus points for a convincing solution

Total points:

Gimme a Gimmick!

Materials

1 cardboard tube

1 plastic spoon

1 empty tissue box

5 cotton balls

3 ping-pong balls

5 paper cups

1 3-ft (0.9-m) length of string

30 drinking straws

1 sheet of mailing labels

Set Up

Place all of the materials on a large table. Provide ample room in which the team can work. Read the list of materials and the team instructions out loud.

Team Instructions

Pillsbury has the doughboy. Oscar Meyer has the Weinermobile. Your task is to create an original, three-dimensional gimmick for a common product that you might find at the grocery store. Your gimmick will then be introduced to the world at a parade. You have seven minutes to build your gimmick and plan a presentation. Your presentation must include a parade announcer telling viewers about the new gimmick and the product it represents. You will be notified when you have three minutes remaining and again when only one minute of planning time remains.

Team Tally

	1	2	3	4	5	6	7	8	9	10
Creativity										
Communication										
Cooperation										

Total points: _____

Emotion Commotion

Materials

    8 small strips of paper
    1 marker or felt-tipped pen
    1 bowl

Set Up

On small strips of paper, write the following words: sad, angry, upset, elated, worried, embarrassed, scared, and joyful. Place the strips of paper in a bowl. Allow ample room in which the team can work. Read the team instructions out loud.

Team Instructions

Our emotions are often visible to others through our body language or facial expressions. In this task, you will have the opportunity to explore some common emotions. Each strip of paper in the bowl has an emotion written on it. You are to take turns choosing a strip of paper out of the bowl and then portraying that emotion. The performer may not speak at any time during the task. The rest of the participants will try to guess the emotion portrayed. You have four minutes to guess as many emotions as possible. You will receive five bonus points for every correctly guessed emotion.

Team Tally

	1	2	3	4	5	6	7	8	9	10
Creativity										
Communication										
Cooperation										

Bonus points: Number of correct guesses _____ x 5 = _____

Total points: _____

9

Trouble with Tasks?

Working Through Some Difficult Spots

In using these tasks over the past several years, I have watched kids blossom as they discover the benefits of teamwork and creativity. I've also encountered a variety of difficulties that temporarily squelched the feeling of teamwork. I have dealt with participants who insist that their way is the best way to solve every task, children who hesitate to jump in and help, grabby kids, unfocused groups, and naysayers who seemed to thrive on telling the team what *wouldn't* work.

Each and every one of these kids had to work at overcoming these individual quirks to become part of a team. For some, it was easy. For others, it was a constant challenge to set aside their own expectations and work within the framework of a group. For all of the kids, it was a lesson in being flexible and working successfully with others.

With trial and error (not to mention a few aspirin!), I've learned some simple tricks for dealing with many of the issues that make teams falter. I've also gleaned many ideas by discussing some common stumbling blocks with other group leaders. Here, you'll find techniques for dealing with some common difficulties as well as suggestions for helping your team members improve their performance.

Bossy Team Members

Overly bossy team members have a tendency to think that their ideas are the only good ones, and they often discount the suggestions of other team members as ridiculous or not worthy of discussion. While strong personalities can benefit groups, those same team members can be the group's downfall if their leadership skills aren't directed in a positive manner. It is crucial that participants understand that every member of the group is equally valuable to the overall effort.

Several things tend to happen with overly aggressive participants. When bossy team members discount the ideas of their teammates and insist that their ideas are the best, the other teammates will begin to assume that the ideas they come up with are invalid and will hesitate to share them. But a task that requires group participation is seldom solved in a stellar manner when only one person on the team is actively working on a solution. A team with more than one strong-willed team member may find itself embroiled in arguments about the best way to solve a task, which wastes valuable planning and building time.

Funneling the energy of overly aggressive team members takes patience, but it is well worth it in the end. In almost all cases, I've found that once these strong participants have learned to step back and allow the entire group the opportunity to participate equally, they are a great asset to the team. Try some of the tactics below to help teams address these bold participants:

- First, remind the entire team that every team member's ideas are valid. Tell the team that laughing at suggestions or commenting negatively about an idea are inappropriate reactions.
- If you find that your team has a number of bossy members who try to outtalk one another, utilize the nonverbal tasks in this book. Preventing aggressive participants from giving orders is a great equalizer.
- Shuffle kids to different places. The group dynamics often change simply by moving kids out of their usual position. If you have two kids with a tendency to take over the planning of tasks, try moving them apart, so that it will be more difficult for them to work together.

- Have a brief discussion time following each team challenge. Ask the teammates what went well, what went wrong, and how they could improve their performance next time. If your team members struggle with an overly aggressive member, they may point out difficulties that arise because of this. They'll likely need some guidance in addressing the situation without being hurtful.

Hesitant Team Members

In stark contrast to their more assertive peers, hesitant children have difficulty sharing ideas with the group and may often spend the duration of the task just watching. These team members need to understand that every idea and every pair of hands on the team is crucial to coming up with the best solution. It may take some time, but once your quiet team members realize that it's safe to share ideas—no matter how unusual they are—they will be more inclined to participate.

Encouraging participation from this type of child can be tricky and might take some time, but these tactics may help:

- As the adult facilitator of the group, make sure to include everyone in team discussions. Address each team member by name, asking for input with regard to how to improve teamwork or solve a problem. Some kids may simply shrug, but asking them for their thoughts shows them that their opinion is valued.
- Try talking about some of the team challenges without attempting to solve them. Read a task aloud and then have the team members offer as many different solutions as they can come up with verbally. You can do this as a free-for-all or work your way around the group, asking each team member his or her thoughts.
- Utilize the tasks in chapter 5. Great for warm-ups, these tasks require verbal discussion, encouraging all members of the group to think and share ideas freely.

Try adjusting some of the tasks to suit your specific needs. Present some of the tasks with limitations: allow only half of the team to talk or assign one person the job of group leader, with the ability to speak and give directions while everyone else remains quiet. Make sure that the quiet participants have a turn to act in the capacity of group leader.

Grabby Kids

It seems like some kids just have to touch things in order to figure them out. Put a pile of interesting building materials like straws, toothpicks, and marshmallows in front of them, and they'll knock down their teammates trying to be the first to grab it all. I've faced this problem with a number of kids on my teams, but it has been a fairly easy obstacle to overcome. In my experience, other participants will object loudly to this kind of behavior, making it a problem you can address quickly and openly. Try some of these tactics when dealing with a grabby child:

- Ask the team members to discuss how a grabby teammate is interfering with their attempts to solve the task
- Remind teams of the time limit—time spent wrestling over materials is time wasted
- Add a new dimension to the task: ask participants to solve the problem with one hand behind their backs or with arms linked
- Challenge grabby children to participate in the task only verbally

Discourage Negativity

Making a judgment about someone's idea before it has had a chance will automatically eliminate any possibilities for improving on that idea and possibly incorporating it into a clever solution. Remind kids that they'll only solve the problem by figuring out what *does* work, and that with team challenges, anything is possible. It is not going to do them any good to have a list of vetoed ideas at the completion of the task.

Teach them that *no* should never be an answer; with team challenges, it is always *yes*. Yes, we could figure out a way to add a purple kangaroo to our presentation. What if he fell into grape juice? Yes, we can use the string as part of our bridge. Maybe instead of a support, it could be a decoration. Yes, we can figure out a way to do it, but we all have to work together.

Mix It Up

It's natural for kids to fall back on what they know. If your group relies on the same person to do the same job during each task, try mixing it up a little. Entice children who are most comfortable in the role of observer to participate by giving them a specific job before the task begins. Ask them to be the timekeeper or to keep track of the specific rules of the task. In this capacity, they must remind their teammates when time is running out or that they need to do each step in a certain manner. If hesitant children know their team is counting on them, they will quickly overcome their hesitancy to participate and realize that they are an asset to the team. Similarly, children who continually insist that their way is the only way to solve a problem will see the ideas of their teammates in a new light when they have the sole responsibility of keeping track of time or specific rules. Of course, this responsibility comes with the caveat that they can't share their ideas with the team!

If you find that your team members solve problems using the same building technique every time (such as creating a tripod base), give them a little nudge toward creative problem-solving skills. Make it mandatory that they use a different method once in a while. For instance, tell the team members who exclusively use the tripod method that a task can be solved using any method *except* a tripod. This pushes them toward more divergent thinking and helps them to come up with new solutions; future projects will benefit from the experience.

If your group members have a tendency to stick with the familiar, you may want to show them one new way to use a particular material after they've completed a task. For instance, if they continue to use sheets of paper only in its flat form, show them how to roll it into a tube to create an entirely different—and stronger—building material. They may even remember the technique next time!

If Your Team Is Still Struggling

After the task is completed, encourage your team members to discuss what might have happened if they had tried other ideas. If time allows, you can even give your group a chance to test other ideas to see how they compare to their original solution.

A great way to make kids more aware of how each individual is contributing to (or detracting from) each solution is to videotape the team. After the task, have the teammates watch the video together. By watching themselves perform, they will be able to pay close attention to trouble spots without the risk of an incomplete task. Be prepared to pause the video! As kids view their attempt at solving a task, have them write down what went wrong, what worked well, and what they would change if they could do the task again. Make it mandatory that, for each negative comment, they must also offer a positive comment. Ask them to discuss how they can use their observations to improve future solutions.

It can sometimes be a struggle to create an environment in which kids feel comfortable sharing outlandish ideas and stretching the limits of their knowledge. However, with patience and understanding—and lots of practice—your group will learn to work together, trust one another, and have fun.

Resources

Creative Problem-Solving Programs for Youth

Craftsman/NSTA Young Inventors Awards Program
National Science Teachers Association
1840 Wilson Boulevard
Arlington, Virginia 22201-3000
(888) 494-4994
E-mail: younginventors@nsta.org
www.nsta.org/programs/craftsman/

Destination ImagiNation
P.O. Box 547
Glassboro, New Jersey 08028
(856) 881-1603
Fax: (856) 881-3596
www.destinationimagination.org
Available internationally

FIRST LEGO League
FIRST (For Inspiration and Recognition of Science and Technology)
200 Bedford Street
Manchester, New Hampshire 03101
(800) 871-8326 or (603) 666-3906, Option 1 for Customer Support
Fax: (603) 666-3907
E-mail: fll@usfirst.org
www.usfirst.org
Available nationally

Future Problem Solving Program
International Office
P.O. Box 23720
Lexington, Kentucky 40523-3720
(800) 256-1499 or (859) 276-4336
Fax: (859) 276-4306
E-mail: mail@fpsp.org
www.fpsp.org
Available internationally

National Engineers Week Future City Competition
Carol Rieg, National Director
1420 King Street
Alexandria, Virginia 22314
(877) 636-9578
Fax: (301) 977-2513
E-mail: cardress@aol.com
www.futurecity.org
Available nationally to middle school students in 7th or 8th grade

National Young Game Inventors Contest
University Games
2030 Harrison Street
San Francisco, California 94110
(415) 503-1600
Fax: (415) 503-0085
E-mail: info@ugames.com
www.ugames.com
Available nationally to individuals or groups

Odyssey of the Mind International
1325 Route 130 S, Suite F
Gloucester City, New Jersey 08030
(856) 456-7776
Fax: (856) 456-7008
E-mail: info@odysseyofthemind.com
www.odysseyofthemind.com
Available internationally

Rube Goldberg Machine Contest
416 N. Chauncey Avenue
West Lafayette, Indiana 47906
E-mail: chairman@rubemachine.com
www.rubemachine.com
A national college-level competition run by Theta Tau Fraternity at
Purdue University in April. Some high school programs are also offered.
Check the Web site for availability.

TOYchallenge
Sally Ride Science
9171 Towne Centre Drive, Suite 550
San Diego, California 92122
(800) 561-5161
E-mail: kristen@sallyridescience.com
www.TOYchallenge.com
Available nationally

Young Inventors Program
Success Beyond the Classroom
4001 Stinson Boulevard, Suite 210
Minneapolis, Minnesota 55421
(612) 638-1516
Fax: (612) 706-0811
E-mail: cmac@ecsu.k12.mn.us
www.successbeyond.org
Available to students and educators in the seven-county metro area of
Minneapolis and St. Paul, Minnesota

About the Author

Kris Bordessa has written for over 50 family and educational publications, including *FamilyFun*, *Home Education Magazine*, *Parenting*, and *Nick Jr. Family Magazine*. She is the author of *Amazing Colonial America Projects You Can Build Yourself* (Nomad Press). Bordessa is also a home educator and an adult volunteer in the 4-H Youth Development and Destination ImagiNation programs. Her Web site is www.krisbordessa.com.